More than words

The hymns of Martin E Leckebusch

This edition published in 2000 by
KEVIN MAYHEW LTD, Buxhall, Stowmarket, Suffolk IP14 3BW

ISBN 1 84003 488 2

Catalogue No 1500325

Cover design by Jonathan Stroulger
Edited by Helen Elliot

Contents

Introduction

Hymns

Remembering my father
Ernest Leckebusch
24 April 1909 - 12 October 1996

and my son
Michael Oliver Leckebusch
12 July 1994 - 7 March 1995

'Savour every moment'

Introduction

The past four decades have seen tremendous changes in the worship life of the English-speaking church. There has been a wealth of fresh material: new texts from the 'hymn explosion', chants and songs from Taizé and Iona, and a great number of songs and choruses from the charismatic/evangelical parts of the church. In addition, the onward march of technology (from photocopiers to word processing to CD-rom and the internet) has made material far more accessible. In all of this there is much for which we can be thankful.

Yet Scripture still urges us to 'sing a *new* song to the Lord' (e.g. Isaiah 42:10): to be made in God's image surely means to be creative. (Imagine how much richer our church life could be, and how much more effective our evangelism, if the energies currently expended on, for example, secular advertising were harnessed for God's service instead!) It is part of our proper response to God to offer him the best we can, not just to repeat what has gone before, so we need the finest of both old *and* new. In addition, intelligent discipleship means applying unchanging truth to a changing world in a way which will genuinely honour God. Hymns and songs which address contemporary issues in the light of both biblical teaching and the traditions of the church remain a valid part of this process of exploring what it means to be God's people today – and tomorrow.

Two concerns

In writing hymn texts, two issues in particular concern me – although, of course, it is for others to judge whether I have addressed them constructively in my texts.

First, *a desire to see hymnody restored* where it has been lost – especially in the charismatic parts of the church, to which I belong. In many congregations hymns have been displaced by worship songs which are rich in intimacy and spontaneity but which tend to equate praise with worship and often focus on a fairly narrow agenda, rarely reaching to the broader issues of discipleship. Christians who have nothing else in their diet may be in a similar position to someone who only eats 'fast food': happy in the short term, but not necessarily well nourished in the long term.

Secondly, *a desire to see the language of worship expanded.* Too often our 'religious' language is alien to outsiders or new Christians.

Even worse, we indulge in a kind of linguistic schizophrenia when we use one set of vocabulary on Sundays (*save, splendour, blessing, cleanse, magnify*) and another (*rescue, brilliance, benefit, wash, applaud*) on Mondays. It is all too easy to divorce faith from daily living!

A personal journey

My own daily life may not be that of a 'typical' hymn writer! I have been a computer systems programmer since 1984, prior to which I read mathematics at Oxford University and took a postgraduate course at Brunel University. I am married with three daughters – our second child, a son, died at eight months – and live in Gloucester.

How did I come to write hymn texts? I was born in 1962 into a family whose roots were basically Methodist, and I regularly attended the local Methodist Sunday School. My personal commitment to Jesus Christ was made when I was 14, at a Pentecostal church to which a school friend had invited me. Over the years my wife and I have attended Pentecostal, Baptist and Methodist churches in different parts of the country – for five years I was a Methodist local preacher – and we are now members of an Anglican congregation.

I began hymn writing almost by accident in 1987. One morning I was studying Psalm 139 and wanted to *sing* it; the only songbook I then possessed contained nothing based on this psalm, so I decided to try to write something. Other texts followed, but it was not until 1994, when I had written just over 100 hymns, that I ventured to send eight texts to Timothy Dudley-Smith for comment. His reply prompted me to revisit and tidy up all I had then written. That process is proving more substantial than I expected: a few texts have required only cosmetic surgery, but most have involved significant reworking and some have been more or less entirely rewritten. (I have been working in alphabetical order, which explains the alphabetical bias of what follows.)

From 1994 to this book is an almost linear progression. Timothy Dudley-Smith put me in touch with the Hymn Society of Great Britain and Ireland, through which I met Caryl Micklem, then Chairman. I sent Caryl a text written for his tune *Gatescarth*; he suggested that I send it to *News of Hymnody*. Ruth Day, then *NoH* editor, drew my attention to Michael Saward's search for material for a proposed Jubilate publication; with only two days to the deadline I therefore had a late night printing texts to send him! Michael passed my name to Churches Together in England for their millennium hymn-book, and it was texts I submitted for that publication which brought my work to Kevin Mayhew's desk . . .

Acknowledgements

There are three main groups of people to thank at this point. Firstly, those named in the preceding paragraph and others who, over the years, have offered various encouragements and criticisms. Particular thanks are due to those at Kevin Mayhew Ltd who have worked hard to make this volume a reality.

Secondly, a number of people have provided the impetus for specific texts, often unwittingly; special thanks are due to Phil Hawkins, Terry Higgins, Adrian Mann, Steve Santry and Graham Vallis, each of whom has initiated at least two texts. Books by Esther de Waal, John Gladwin and Colin Urquhart have also spurred more than one text each. I am also grateful to Ian Sharp for some excellent new tunes which he has written for a few of the texts.

Finally, my thanks are due to Jane, my wife, who has often tempered my enthusiasm with realism and wisdom, who has offered both specific advice and general encouragement, and whose support in word and deed has been invaluable.

Notes on the texts

The texts in this book are printed in alphabetical order of first line, not of title. Tunes are suggested for many texts; other suggestions would be welcome, especially, of course, for those texts which have unusual metres for which no tune yet exists. An asterisk (∗) denotes a tune which can be used only by combining or dividing verses of the text. Appendix C indicates a number of books in which the majority of the suggested tunes can be found.

There are also several *indexes:*
- The texts are cross-referenced to the *Subject Index* to allow quick reference to other texts on the same major themes. Texts are typically included in three sections of this subject index.

- The *Thematic Index* gives keyword references to texts and supplements the subject index. In many cases, the word in question is found in the texts listed; often, though, the theme word touches on an underlying aspect of the text rather than its actual vocabulary. (For example, four texts are referenced here with the word *Bible;* none contains that word, though all have some reference to Scripture.)

- A *Scriptural Index* is provided. Biblical references are included on the texts themselves only where the text has arisen from considering the verses in question. Often the Scriptural reference is an allusion rather than a quotation, and may refer to only part of the verse(s) cited.

- The *Church Year Index* lists texts relating to the major seasons of the Christian calendar.

- A *Metrical Index* is included. This index also lists the suggested tunes for each beat.

- Finally, the *Index of Titles and First Lines* includes titles (in italics) only where they differ from the first line of the text.

A note on *inclusive language* may be appropriate. Although I come from a conservative theological position and am happy to talk of God in traditional masculine language (as reflected in many of the texts) I recognise that some Christians find themselves less comfortable with such usage. For some texts, where minor amendments can remove such references, I therefore offer inclusive language variations (see Appendix A) which may be used in place of the standard text. Requests for other alterations should be addressed to the publisher.

And finally . . .

These texts are offered in the hope that they will enrich the worship life of the church, help Christ's people in their discipleship and thereby bring glory to God – alone.

Then Let Us Go

1 A broken loaf – this broken world
   sees many starve, deprived of bread:
   Such vast inequities remain –
   some spoilt for choice, some underfed.
   A broken loaf – to Jesus' feast
   we come as equals, drawn by grace;
      then let us go, resolved anew
      to make this world a fairer place.

2 A common cup – in wine like this
   some seek delight, some lose control;
   yet those whom evil snares and scars
   by Christ are made both free and whole.
   A common cup – we see afresh
   that everything Christ had, he gave;
      then let us go, empowered by love
      to serve the world he died to save.

Subject Index: H4, I6, J1
8 8 8 8 D (DLM)
Suggested Tunes: *Addison's (London); Jerusalem*

We Lift Our Hearts in Worship

1 Across the boundless breadth of space,
   assigning every star its place,
   Lord God, your sovereign hand we trace –
      and offer you our worship.

2 Your vast design is evident
   on every isle and continent
   where nature, so luxuriant,
      inspires our hearts to worship.

3 You fashion rain and frost and snow,
   make sun to blaze and wind to blow,
   till garden, field and forest grow –
      with thankful hearts we worship.

4 So many species, formed to fill
   both sea and air, both plain and hill!
   For all your rich creative skill
      we lift our hearts in worship.

5 Can our lives then elude your sight?
   Your love sustains us day and night!
   To you, our Saviour, Lord, Delight,
      we gladly bring our worship.

Subject Index: A2, F2, J2
888 7
Suggested Tune: *Lord of Love*
See also Appendix A

Piercing Thorns

1 A crown of piercing thorns
   they forced upon your head:
   to claim and cleanse my selfish mind
   your precious blood was shed.

2 The flesh upon your back
   their brutal scourging tore:
   how can I shirk another's load
   since you my burden bore?

3 Lord, how can I forget
   the nail-prints in your hands?
   Make me a servant of your grace,
   fulfilling love's demands.

4 Your feet they firmly held
   as nails were hammered through:
   my feet are free – but how can I
   not choose to follow you?

5 The spear which broke your side
   made blood and water flow;
   come, pierce my heart, that through my life
   your suffering love may show.

6 You took my place in death,
   your blood was freely poured:
   then let my life be spent for you,
   my Saviour and my Lord!

Subject Index: B4, F5, H6
6 6 8 6 (SM)
Suggested Tune: *St Thomas*

4

The Finest Fruit

1 A depth of satisfaction:
   the promise is made known
   to all who turn from evil
   and make the Lord their own;
      who heed no wicked counsel,
      no cynic's mocking voice;
      whose way of living signals
      obedience as their choice.

2 The man or woman choosing
   to follow what is right
   will find God's word becoming
   a source of pure delight:
      here meditation causes
      the finest fruit to grow
      as when a tree is planted
      where streams of water flow.

3 To trust in God will give us
   a grounding firm and sure;
   to disregard his wisdom
   would make us insecure;
      Lord, let us not be worthless
      like chaff that blows away –
      but guide us and protect us;
      watch over us each day.

Psalm 1
Subject Index: E, F1, H6
7 6 7 6 D
Suggested Tunes: *Crüger* (Herrnhut); *Ellacombe*
See also Appendix A

A Race to Run

1 Ahead of us, a race to run:
    so, looking at the past no more,
    forgetting what has gone before,
we fix our eyes on God the Son –
    with eager diligence we train
    as for the prize ahead we strain
until at last our course is done.

2 He calls us now to run the race,
    discarding every weight and load
    to speed our way along the road;
the path we tread, the way of grace –
    and though the journey may be long
    the grace of God will keep us strong
until we stand before his face.

Hebrews 12:1-2; Philippians 3:13-14;
1 Corinthians 9:25; Isaiah 40:31
Subject Index: F5, H6, I4
8 88 8 88 8
Suggested Tune: by Andrew Griffith

6

To the Lamb

1 All power to the Lamb of God:
   he wore the robes of servanthood
   and in the place of weakness stood –
   all power to the Lamb!

2 All riches to the Lamb of God
   who came among us, one so poor,
   to make us rich for evermore –
   all riches to the Lamb!

3 All wisdom to the Lamb of God
   who chose the way of suffering:
   to status he refused to cling –
   all wisdom to the Lamb!

4 And to the Lamb of God, all strength:
   his love was strong enough to win,
   defeating all the might of sin –
   and to the Lamb, all strength!

5 All honour to the Lamb of God
   who laid his honour far aside
   when on a cross of shame he died –
   all honour to the Lamb!

6 All glory to the Lamb of God:
   his name above all others now;
   let every knee before him bow –
   all glory to the Lamb!

7 All praises to the Lamb of God,
   for he is worthy, who was slain,
   who now and evermore shall reign –
   all praises to the Lamb!

Revelation 5:12; Philippians 2:6-11; 2 Corinthians 8:9
Subject Index: B4, F3, J4
8 88 6
Suggested Tune: *Childhood*

The Voice of God

1 Amid the clamour of the world
   the voice of God is heard:
   the ear that has been taught by faith
   can recognise his word.

2 For through the chequered history
   of this rebellious race
   obliquely, using human tongues,
   the Lord has promised grace.

3 And yet to speak more plainly still
   he made our life his own:
   most clearly in the Son of Man
   the Word of God is known.

4 He still reveals the truth to all
   who truly want to learn –
   who in their life-experience
   the hand of God discern.

5 This is no mere philosophy,
   but all the tools of life;
   his Spirit speaks the holy word
   in all our joy and strife.

6 Equip us, Lord, to face the needs
   confronting us today
   with wisdom to perceive your call
   and courage to obey.

Subject Index: A2, E, J2
8 6 8 6 (CM)
Suggested Tune: *Albano*

Look Ahead

1 At this table we remember
   how and where our faith began:
   in the pain of crucifixion
   suffered by the Son of Man.

2 Looking up in adoration
   faith is conscious – he is here!
   Christ is present with his people,
   his the call that draws us near.

3 Heart and mind we each examine:
   if with honesty we face
   all our doubt, our fear and failure,
   then we can receive his grace.

4 Peace we share with one another:
   as from face to face we turn
   in our brothers and our sisters
   Jesus' body we discern.

5 Bread and wine are set before us;
   as we eat, we look ahead:
   we shall dine with Christ in heaven
   where the Kingdom feast is spread.

6 Nourished by the bread of heaven,
   faith and strength and courage grow –
   so to witness, serve and suffer,
   out into the world we go.

Subject Index: H6, I6, J4
8 7 8 7
Suggested Tunes: *Stuttgart; Love Divine*

The Frontier

1 A universe of rich delights
with much to thrill the questing mind –
and yet, in each experience,
     new challenges we find:
for moral choices multiply,
and where uncertainties are rife
we feel the lure of easy ways
     which undervalue life.

2 Immense dilemmas still remain
whatever forward steps we take,
for new solutions often raise
     new questions in their wake.
Lord, give us courage not to dodge
the issues which confront our race,
but may we name with honesty
     the problems which we face.

3 So many fresh discoveries
as science searches paths unknown –
and yet the source of each advance
     is found in you alone.
To all who tread the frontier
where study broadens human skill,
Lord, grant the wisdom to pursue
your wisdom and your will.

Subject Index: A2, H3, J2
8 8 8 6 D
Suggested Tunes: *Framlingham; Childhood**

Before a Crown

1 Before a crown, a cross to bear:
   with Jesus we are crucified;
   he calls us now to put to death
   our selfish dreams and empty pride.

2 And in this world which killed the Lord,
   his path of suffering we must share:
   like him, we may be scorned or cursed –
   before a crown, a cross to bear.

3 But from the cross, a crown to wear:
   we gladly walk our pilgrim way,
   rejoice to know our risen Lord
   and live to serve him every day.

4 We soon shall see the King enthroned
   in majesty beyond compare;
   we may encounter trials on earth –
   but from the cross, a crown to wear.

Subject Index: H6, I2, J4
8 8 8 8 (LM)
Suggested Tunes: *Angelus; O Righteous Lord*

Be Strong

1 Be strong in Jesus, the crucified,
   exalted now at the Father's side:
   he died in weakness, but now he lives,
   and strengthens us by the help he gives.
   His death provides for our liberty,
   we share his glorious victory –
   be strong, be strong in the Lord!

2 Be strong in Jesus, the one who saves –
   who offers freedom where sin enslaves.
   Though death held sway ever since the fall
   the gift of Jesus is life for all:
   his Spirit comes as a guarantee
   of our eternal security –
   be strong, be strong in the Lord!

3 Be strong, though trouble is often near;
   with Christ to help us, we need not fear:
   he always promises ample grace
   for all the trials we have to face –
   and heaven's glories will far outweigh
   whatever problems are ours today –
   be strong, be strong in the Lord!

4 Be strong, for Jesus has won the fight:
   the powers of darkness he put to flight!
   Declare allegiance to him alone –
   and then his triumph will be your own,
   for God intends us to share his reign –
   our faithful service is not in vain –
   be strong, be strong in the Lord!

2 Timothy 2:1; 2 Corinthians 1:21-22, 13:4;
Ephesians 1:20, 6:10; 1 Corinthians 10:13, 15:57-58;
Galatians 5:1; Romans 5:17, 8:18; John 16:33; James 4:7-8
Subject Index: G2, H5, I4
99 99 99 7

Free to Live

1 Born of Adam's rebel race,
   captives in the grasp of sin,
   when we tried to keep God's law
   we could fight but seldom win;
   yet, because of Jesus' death,
   we are made completely new:
   changed beyond our wildest dreams,
   counted righteous through and through!

2 Sheltered by the cross of Christ,
   our position is secure;
   in the Son the Father loves
   we are hidden evermore.
   Nowhere safer could we find:
   God himself has placed us here –
   such acceptance draws the sting
   from our deepest guilt and fear.

3 Since we share his risen life
   in the strength of Christ we stand:
   we can make his triumph ours
   when temptation is at hand.
   Crucified and raised with Christ,
   no more trapped in Adam's race –
   God declares us free to live,
   to enjoy abundant grace!

Subject Index: B4, H1, I3
7 7 7 7 D
Suggested Tune: *Hollingside*

Ocean's Limits

1 Broader than the ocean's limits –
lost horizon, distant shore –
how the love of God engulfs us
now and evermore!

2 Stronger than the strongest current,
surer than the coming tide –
peace, the promise of salvation,
reaches far and wide.

3 Deeper than the darkest caverns
hidden far beneath the sea –
deeper still is God's forgiveness:
lasting, full and free.

4 Mighty is the swell that surges,
awesome are the crashing waves;
stronger yet is our Deliverer –
praise the God who saves!

Subject Index: A4, G1, J1
8 7 8 5
Suggested Tunes: *Griffin's Brook; St Leonard's* (Gould)

Royal Priesthood

1 By the sacrifice of Jesus –
   body broken, blood outpoured –
   we are made forever holy,
   free to stand before the Lord:
     Christ as Saviour we confess –
     he is all our righteousness.

2 Though we once were godless sinners,
   gone are all our guilt and shame;
   we are chosen, cleansed, acquitted,
   justified in Jesus' name;
     held within his constant care
     in his kingdom now we share.

3 Called to be a royal priesthood
   praising God in life and song,
   built into a living temple,
   to each other we belong;
     so together now we bring
     thankful worship to our King.

Hebrews 10:10, 14; 1 Corinthians 1:30, 6:11; 1 Peter 2:9;
Ephesians 2:21; Romans 12:5
Subject Index: B4, H1, I2
8 7 8 7 77
Suggested Tunes: *Latvia; All Saints*

Every Day in Every Place

1 Called by Christ to be disciples
   every day in every place,
   we are not to hide as hermits
   but to spread the way of grace;
      citizens of heaven's kingdom,
      though this world is where we live,
      as we serve a faithful Master,
      faithful service may we give.

2 Richly varied are our pathways,
   many callings we pursue:
   may we use our gifts and talents
   always, Lord, to honour you;
      so in government or commerce,
      college, hospice, farm or home,
      whether volunteers or earning,
      may we see your kingdom come.

3 Hard decisions may confront us,
   urging us to compromise;
   still obedience is our watchword –
   Father, make us strong and wise!
      Secular is turned to sacred,
      made a precious offering,
      as our daily lives are fashioned
      in submission to our King.

Subject Index: H6, I2, J2
8 7 8 7 D
Suggested Tunes: *Hyfrydol; Alleluia*
See also Appendix A

Children of God

1 Children of God himself –
   children he calls his own!
   Ours is a way of peace
   previously unknown:
   the Spirit's leading makes us free
   for all that we were meant to be.

2 'Abba, our Father God!'
   Cry from our heart of hearts;
   pledges that we are his
   tenderly he imparts,
   so we are merely echoing
   the truth the Spirit comes to bring.

3 Each of us now his child,
   each of us made an heir:
   chosen with Christ our Lord,
   all that is his to share,
   for those who share his sufferings
   will reign with him, the King of kings.

Romans 8:14-17
Subject Index: A5, H2, I3
6 6 6 6 88
Suggested Tune: *Little Cornard*
See also Appendix B

Come to the Kingdom

1 Christ brings the kingdom where barrenness blooms:
    see how the image of God is restored,
yielding a harvest of talents and skills
    when we acknowledge our Maker as Lord.

2 Come to his kingdom of weakness made strong,
    brokenness mended, the blind given sight;
welcome and dignity crown the despised,
    darkness is banished by glorious light.

3 Come to his kingdom where righteousness reigns –
    God has commanded: repent and believe!
Children of dust in his glory may share,
    penitent rebels his favour receive.

4 Come to his kingdom of laughter and hope,
    savour the freedom its fullness will bring:
no more oppression, injustice or fear –
    come to the kingdom where Jesus is King!

Isaiah 35:1, 3, 8, 10
Subject Index: G2, I2, J1
10 10 10 10
Suggested Tunes: *Chedworth; Gasquet Hall; Slane*
See also Appendix A

In the Fight

1 Christian soldiers in the fight
    wrestling evil forces,
    great are our resources!
  Mighty armour God provides:
    using every section
    gives us full protection.

2 As a belt we take the truth,
    trusting God to save us
    by the truth he gave us.
  What a breastplate: God himself
    tells us how he sees us –
    righteous in Christ Jesus!

3 Now we wear the gospel shoes,
    everywhere declaring
    peace that is for sharing;
when we raise the shield of faith
    how can Satan harm us?
    He will not alarm us!

4 Gift of God to bring our minds
    into liberation:
    helmet of salvation!
  Such a powerful sword to wield:
    how God's word inspires us!
    How his Spirit fires us!

5 When we pray, the Spirit's voice
    whispers deep inside us,
    speaking words to guide us:
  God has pledged to bring us through,
    in his strength abounding –
    all our foes confounding!

Ephesians 6:11-18
Subject Index: H5, I4
7 66 D
Suggested Tune: *Cuckfield*

Christ Is Our Freedom

1 Christ is our freedom: Christ who is Lord
   shared in our life and died in our place.
   Now he has paid the price for our sin,
   clearing the way for pardon and grace:
   holiness we could never achieve
   comes as a gift to all who believe!

2 Christ is our freedom: there at the cross
   he tore apart the shackles of sin:
   now he has set the hostages free,
   now resurrection life can begin.
   Once we were slaves to sin and its powers –
   now we are Christ's, and freedom is ours.

3 Christ is our freedom: Christ is alive!
   Though he was dead, in triumph he rose!
   Into his Church his Spirit he pours,
   bringing his life as through us he flows –
   we can enjoy the promised release:
   lifted from guilty struggling to peace.

4 Christ is our freedom: baptism tells
   what he has done, and what he will give:
   buried with Christ, to him we belong;
   he is our life – for him we now live,
   trusting his promise, born of his word,
   freed to be fruitful serving the Lord.

Romans 3:22, 24, 25; 1 Peter 3:18; Romans 6:5-7;
2 Corinthians 5:17; John 7:37; Romans 8:1-2, 6:3-4;
Galatians 2:20; 1 Peter 1:23; Romans 7:4; John 15:8
Subject Index: B4, H1, I5
9 9 9 9 99

Christ Is Our Peace!

1 Christ is our peace! For Christ himself
   brought us together, made us one:
   in him our barriers are destroyed –
   all our hostilities are gone.

2 Christ is our peace! Throughout his life
   ours was the heavy load he bore;
   rituals that failed to nourish faith
   he has abolished evermore.

3 Christ is our peace! For in his death
   our broken past is left behind;
   now he fulfils his solemn pledge:
   new life and hope for humankind.

4 Christ is our peace! For by the cross
   he guarantees the way of grace:
   peace with each other and with God,
   gifts to an undeserving race.

5 Christ is our peace! Across the world
   Father and Son and Spirit call:
   we can enjoy a welcome home –
   God's invitation reaches all.

Ephesians 2:14-18
Subject Index: B4, G2, I2
8 8 8 8 (LM)
Suggested Tune: *Duke Street*
See also Appendix B

A Greater Glory

1 Christ our Lord, we worship you,
   for you left eternal glory,
   taking mortal flesh and blood,
   born to share our human story;
   hallelujah!

2 Some who climbed a mountain high
   glimpsed the truth – and fell, dumbfounded:
   was your honour not disclosed
   when the Father's voice resounded?
   Hallelujah!

3 Yet a greater glory shone
   when you faced humiliation,
   when you suffered in our place,
   crucified for our salvation;
   hallelujah!

4 And your resurrection proved
   sin's oppressive grasp was ended,
   for you rose as living Lord
   and in triumph you ascended;
   hallelujah!

5 What a hope we now possess,
   far surpassing earthly measure
   for your Spirit thrills our hearts
   with a taste of heaven's treasure!
   Hallelujah!

6 When in splendour you return
   every knee shall bow before you!
   Come, our King, and take your throne –
   hallelujah! We adore you!
   Hallelujah!

Subject Index: B6, F3, J3
7 8 7 8 4
Suggested Tune: *St Albinus*
See also Appendix A

Come and See

1 Come and see what the Lord has revealed –
see a man so familiar with grief:
one whose face is disfigured and bruised,
one whose sufferings allow no relief.

2 See the anguish and woe that he bears –
what a burden to carry alone!
And we thought him afflicted by God,
never dreaming the load was our own.

3 See him pierced, see him crushed for our sin –
he was punished to bring us release:
we had all turned away from the truth;
he was scorned and abused for our peace.

4 And in silence he patiently stood
in the midst of oppression and strife:
for our hatred, our violence and lies
there he paid with the price of his life.

5 Yet the will of the Lord can be seen
in the painful ordeal he endured,
for the freedom his people enjoy
is the prize that his death has secured.

6 Come and see what the Lord has revealed –
see his Servant enthroned evermore,
for he poured out his life unto death
and the cost of salvation he bore.

Isaiah 53:1-12
Subject Index: B4, G2, I6
9 9 9 9
Suggested Tune: *Cottingham*

Come, Praise

1 Come, praise the Lord, all you nations:
  come, praise the Lord, come to worship and adore
  and exalt his name – he is worthy
    to be praised,
    to be praised,
  to be praised for evermore.

2 Come, meet the Lord, all you peoples:
  come and rejoice, for his love for you is great
  and his faithfulness is unending –
    bless the Lord,
    bless the Lord,
  bless the Lord, and celebrate!

Psalm 117
Subject Index: A2, F1, J1
8 11 9 33 7

Breathtaking Splendour

1 Come, see the Lord in his breathtaking splendour:
gaze at his majesty – bow and adore!
Enter his presence with wonder and worship –
he is the King, and enthroned evermore.

2 He is the Word who was sent by the Father,
born as a baby, a child of our race:
God here among us, revealed as a servant,
walking the pathway of truth and of grace.

3 He is the Lamb who was slain to redeem us –
there at the cross his appearance was marred;
though he emerged from the grave as the victor,
still from the nails and the spear he is scarred.

4 He is the Lord who ascended in triumph –
ever the sound of his praises shall ring!
Hail him the First and the Last, the Almighty:
Jesus, our Prophet, our Priest and our King.

5 Come, see the Lord in his breathtaking splendour:
gaze at his majesty – bow and adore!
Come and acknowledge him Saviour and Sovereign:
Jesus our King is enthroned evermore.

Subject Index: B1, F2, J4
11 10 11 10
Suggested Tunes: *Barnard Gate; Epiphany*

Endless Care

1 Come with thanks to offer to the Lord;
  bring your praises, honouring his name!
    You he redeemed out of every land,
    come with your songs of his mighty hand –
  tell of the freedom you now enjoy;
  his saving mercy and power proclaim!

2 You who found yourselves without a home –
  in an empty wilderness you strayed! –
    tell of the Lord who became your guide
    when in confusion for help you cried;
  now you are walking a different way,
  home to the city that God has made.

3 Those of you who shunned the Lord's commands,
  tasting only bitterness and strife:
    though you rebelled and despised his word,
    when you repented your prayer was heard;
  sing of the riches he gave you then:
  pardon for sin, and eternal life.

4 You whose lives were battered by the storms,
  tossed in turmoil on a raging sea:
    where could you turn in your fear and grief,
    give up your anguish, and find relief?
  Come and rejoice in the God whose power
  brought you to land and security.

5 Now you know the favour of the Lord,
  his eternal promises you share;
    know that if trouble should visit you
    God will be with you to bring you through:
  ponder the ways of your Lord and King –
  praise him because of his endless care!

Psalm 107
Subject Index: F1, G2, H7
9 9 99 9 9

Wounded Healer

1 Come, wounded Healer, your sufferings reveal –
   the scars you accepted, our anguish to heal.
       Your wounds bring such comfort in body and soul
       to all who bear torment and yearn to be whole.

2 Come, hated Lover, and gather us near,
   your welcome, your teaching, your challenge to hear:
       where scorn and abuse cause rejection and pain,
       your loving acceptance makes hope live again!

3 Come, broken Victor, condemned to a cross –
   how great are the treasures we gain from your loss!
       Your willing agreement to share in our strife
       transforms our despair into fullness of life.

Subject Index: B1, F5, H2
10 11 11 11
Suggested Tunes: *Deepcar; Slane*

Creation Sings!

1 Creation sings! Each plant and tree,
   each bird and beast in harmony;
   the brightest star, the smallest cell,
   God's tender care and glory tell –
   from ocean depths to mountain peaks,
   in praise of God, creation speaks!

2 Creation speaks a message true,
   reminds us we are creatures, too:
   to serve as stewards is our role,
   despite our dreams of full control –
   when we disparage what God owns,
   in turmoil, all creation groans.

3 Creation groans to see the day
   which ends all bondage, all decay:
   frustrated now, it must await
   the Lord who comes to recreate
   till round the universe there rings
   the song his new creation sings!

Subject Index: A2, J4
88 88 88
Suggested Tunes: *The Vines; Melita*
See also Appendix A

Do You Not Know?

1 Do you not know? This is our God!
   Were you not told his holy name?
   Have you not heard? He is the Lord,
   age after age ever the same.

2 To whom will you compare the Lord,
   the God no image can portray?
   No artist has sufficient skill,
   his might or glory to display.

3 Beyond the earth, beyond the skies,
   he reigns, enthroned as King of all;
   though earthly rulers flaunt their power,
   at his command their empires fall.

4 Who is there like the Holy One?
   And who can fathom his design?
   The planets' orbits he decrees,
   and causes sun and stars to shine.

5 How can you worry that your God
   might choose to disregard your prayer?
   He neither slumbers nor forgets,
   and you enjoy his constant care.

6 So trust the everlasting Lord
   your failing vigour to renew –
   then you shall soar on eagles' wings,
   with God himself sustaining you.

Isaiah 40:18-31
Subject Index: A2, H2
8 8 8 8 (LM)
Suggested Tunes: *Church Triumphant; Jerusalem**

All Splendour and All Majesty

1 Eternal God, we bring our praise
   to you, our Father and our Friend;
   to you, whose word has never failed,
      whose reign shall never end:
   all greatness and all power are yours,
   all splendour and all majesty –
   for over heaven and earth you rule
      with total sovereignty.

2 Your kingdom stands for evermore –
   enthroned on high, you are the King!
   Let every tongue acknowledge you
      as Lord of everything.
   Our wealth and honour come from you;
   from you are strength and power and fame;
   how glad we are to give you thanks
      and magnify your name.

3 But who are we to worship you,
   to make our offerings at your throne?
   Whatever gifts we choose to bring
      have come from you alone.
   Let all that we possess be yours –
   ourselves, our lives, our riches too;
   confessing you as Lord and God
      we bow and honour you!

1 Chronicles 29:10-14
Subject Index: A5, F2, H4
8 8 8 6 D
Suggested Tunes: *Framlingham; Childhood**

Father, How Glad

1 Father, how glad I am to be your child,
   drawn by your love, restored and reconciled,
   called to a glory none may yet foresee:
   the likeness of your Son, made known in me.

2 Father, how glad I am that Jesus came,
   taking my sin and shouldering the blame;
   conscious that I am pardoned evermore,
   how could I keep on sinning like before?

3 Father, how glad I am that Jesus rose,
   sealing his triumph over all his foes:
   now Satan's stratagems are doomed to fail –
   now all who place their trust in you prevail!

4 Father, how glad I am to walk your way,
   glad of your Spirit's teaching day by day –
   and, with a deep assurance born of grace,
   how glad that I shall see you face to face.

1 John 3:1-9, 2:28-29
Subject Index: A5, F4, H2
10 10 10 10
Suggested Tune: *Go Forth*

Gracious Reign

1 For believing hearts, a gift
  far beyond imagining
  as the Spirit makes his home
  where the Son of God is King:
    welcome now the gracious reign
    which the Spirit comes to bring.

2 Though our bodies face decay
  as a consequence of sin,
  yet our spirits are aglow
  from the risen Christ within –
    where the Spirit works in power
    resurrection can begin!

3 We can disregard the claims
  of a nature which has died,
  for the Spirit takes control,
  putting selfishness aside –
    we are children of the Lord
    and his Spirit is our guide.

Romans 8:9-14
Subject Index: C, H1, I1
7 7 7 7 7 7
Suggested Tune: *Dix*
See also Appendix B

32

But Most of All We Thank You

1 For every word which feeds us
    by nourishing the soul,
which satisfies our hunger
    and makes our spirits whole;
for milk and meat, we thank you,
    for strength to face the fight;
for truth which we can savour,
    our comfort and delight;
for Scriptures which were written
    by those your Spirit stirred –
but most of all we thank you
    for Christ, the living Word!

2 For bread which speaks so clearly
    of all that you have done
and wine which tells the anguish
    by which our peace was won;
for all that spells forgiveness,
    a pardon for the past;
for hope which we can cherish,
    a promise which will last;
we thank you for the table
    where such a feast is spread –
but most of all we thank you
    for Christ, the living Bread!

Subject Index: E, F4, I6
7 6 7 6 Triple
Suggested Tune: *Thaxted*

Give Thanks

1 For riches of salvation
        give thanks to the Lord;
    release from condemnation,
        give thanks to the Lord;
    for love which truly frees us
    because the Father sees us
    identified with Jesus –
        give thanks, give thanks to the Lord!

2 For courage and endurance
        give thanks to the Lord;
    the Spirit's reassurance,
        give thanks to the Lord;
    for fatherly correction,
    the call to share perfection,
    the hope of resurrection –
        give thanks, give thanks to the Lord!

3 For life in all its fullness
        give thanks to the Lord;
    for all that leads to wholeness
        give thanks to the Lord;
    he knows our every feeling
    and speaks in grace, revealing
    his comfort and his healing –
        give thanks, give thanks to the Lord!

4 For justice with compassion
        give thanks to the Lord,
    and freedom from oppression
        give thanks to the Lord;
    for holiness unending,
    a kingdom still extending,
    all earthly power transcending –
        give thanks, give thanks to the Lord!

Subject Index: F4, H6, J2
7 5 7 5 777 7
Suggested Tune: *Burgess Hill*
See also Appendix A

Threshold of the Years

1 For the courage and conviction
  seen in saints of other days,
  for the treasures which they left us,
  Father, hear our grateful praise:
  like a tree in all its splendour,
  full of life, mature and strong,
  is this heritage we cherish –
  and in which we now belong.

2 Like a swiftly-flowing river,
  hours and minutes slip away,
  while the ever-changing seasons
  chart renewal and decay:
  give us grace to seize each moment,
  wisdom to perceive its worth,
  and your Spirit's promised guidance
  every day we walk this earth.

3 Help us, Lord, to shape a future
  grounded in community –
  like a vibrant, growing city,
  rich with opportunity.
  Teach us how to stand together,
  sharing hopes, transcending fears,
  as we meet tomorrow's challenge
  on the threshold of the years.

4 Yet by faith we see a prospect
  mortal sight can never know,
  where the trees provide for healing,
  where the living waters flow:
  this is your eternal city,
  one no human power could build;
  Jesus, come! We seek your kingdom –
  glimpsed on earth, in heaven fulfilled.

Subject Index: F5, H6, J1
8 7 8 7 D
Suggested Tunes: *Hope Park; Abbot's Leigh*

Freedom, We Pray

1 Freedom, we pray,
    for the poor and oppressed –
for the victims of tyranny,
    crying out for rest;
Lord, hear our prayer:
    let injustice and torture cease;
let the power of brutality
    yield to the power of peace!

2 Still we admit
    we are conscious of sin –
of the self-centred attitudes
    lurking deep within;
open our hearts
    to the pardon and grace we need,
to the truth of the Son of God,
    till we are free indeed.

3 Lord, hear our cry
    for a world gone astray
as we look for a brighter hope
    in the coming Day;
stir us to strive
    for a freedom unknown before
till the kingdom's fulfilment brings
    freedom for evermore.

Subject Index: G2, H3, J1
4 6 8 5 4 8 8 6
Suggested Tune: *Hymn to Freedom* (Oscar Peterson, adapted)

Our Hope, Our Refuge Be

1 From age to age, Lord, you endure:
   from long before the earth,
   before you made the mountain peaks
   or brought this world to birth;
      from everlasting you are God,
      to all eternity:
      for evermore you are our Lord –
      our hope, our refuge be!

2 We tremble at your holiness,
   for we are merely clay;
   Almighty God, your awesome power
   could sweep our lives away.
      Although we try to hide our sins,
      to you our guilt is clear –
      but by your mercy may we learn
      to live in godly fear.

3 To you a thousand years are like
   a day, an hour gone by,
   but we are like the morning grass:
   by evening, frail and dry –
      so teach us how to weigh our lives,
      to number all our days,
      and by your timeless wisdom, Lord,
      instruct us in your ways.

4 With songs of gladness fill our hearts;
   let love adorn our years;
   and may unending peace assuage
   the past, with all its tears.
      To us and to our children show
      your saving majesty:
      from age to age, Lord, prosper us –
      our hope, our refuge be!

Psalm 90
Subject Index: A3, F1, H6
8 6 8 6 D (DCM)
Suggested Tune: *St Matthew*

Messiah Will Appear

1 From ancient times the promise stood:
  Messiah would appear!
  The eager prophets yearned to see
  the mystery made clear;
  but though they faithfully proclaimed
  such truth as they could see,
  how far beyond their greatest hopes
  fulfilment was to be!

2 For God the Son was born on earth
  and took a human frame;
  in mortal flesh and blood and bone
  the promised Saviour came:
  so, nourished by a mother's milk,
  his earthly life began:
  the sovereign Lord of all became
  the infant Son of Man.

3 The promised kingdom he revealed
  to any who believed,
  and hundreds, from his tender power,
  a healing touch received;
  yet we condemned him to a cross –
  Messiah crucified! –
  and there, to free the human race,
  he suffered, bled and died.

4 Now seated at his Father's side
  he will return to reign:
  the one who once was born a babe
  as King will come again.
  The climax of our history,
  the awesome day, draws near
  when, making good his ancient pledge,
  Messiah will appear!

Subject Index: B2, G2, J3
8 6 8 6 D (DCM)
Suggested Tunes: *Northover; Kingsfold; Noel*

On Your Mercy

1 From the depths my soul cries out:
 listen, Lord, to my plea;
 on your mercy I depend –
 hear my cry and answer me.

2 If you kept a list of sins
 who could stand free of blame?
 But forgiveness comes from you –
 therefore I revere your name.

3 More than those who watch at night
 for the coming of day –
 more than this my eager soul
 waits to hear what you will say.

4 Lord, may those who seek your love
 find you faithful and true;
 may your endless mercies reach
 all who put their hope in you.

Psalm 130
Subject Index: F1, G2, H3
7 6 7 7
Suggested Tune: *Sutton Manor*

Praise the Living Lord

1 Give glory to Jesus
whose rising from the dead
surpasses fulfilment
of all the prophets said:
    from days of old
    their words foretold
    his anguish and his reign –
    he died, and rose again,
so praise the Living Lord!

2 Give glory to Jesus
who lives for evermore,
by whose vindication
we know we stand secure:
    our debt is cleared,
    and all we feared
    now shrivels in the light
    of love's triumphant might –
so praise the Living Lord!

3 Give glory to Jesus
who reigns as gracious Lord,
transforming the future
through broken lives restored:
    from hearts ablaze
    with love and praise
    we yearn to do his will –
    so now with all our skill
we praise our Living Lord!

Subject Index: B5, F3, H1
6 6 6 6 44 66 6
Suggested Tune: *Symphony No 1* (Johannes Brahms, adapted)

Give Me a Heart

1 Give me a heart that will honour you:
   in willing submission before your throne,
   ambitions and plans to be yours alone;
 give me a heart that will honour you:
   will follow the way to the Saviour's cross,
   accepting the challenge of pain and loss –
 O give me a heart, a heart that will honour you.

2 Give me a heart that will honour you:
   a heart that is rich in humility,
   a heart that will worship eternally;
 give me a heart that will honour you:
   no more can my emptiness stay concealed –
   my twisted emotions to you I yield;
 O give me a heart, a heart that will honour you.

3 Give me a heart that will honour you,
   rejecting the dazzle of wealth and fame,
   continually living to praise your name;
 give me a heart that will honour you
   where patience and kindness can freely grow,
   enabling the power of your love to flow –
 O give me a heart, a heart that will honour you.

Subject Index: F5, H1
9 10 10 9 10 10 12

Marvellous Gift

1 Give thanks to the Lord for his marvellous gift:
the Son born on earth as a child of our race,
the Wonderful Counsellor, Prince of all peace –
incredible gift of immeasurable grace.

2 For such was the depth of the love of the Lord,
he gave us his Son, at unspeakable cost –
the riches of heaven he willingly spent
fulfilling his yearning to rescue the lost.

3 Remember the grace of our Lord Jesus Christ:
the path of the humblest of servants he trod;
from heaven he stooped to the shame of a cross
to win our salvation and bring us to God.

4 Now God has exalted this Jesus on high –
how great is the glory bestowed on his name:
let all of creation confess him as Lord –
to him be all honour, all praise and acclaim!

5 So let us consider the kindness of God –
what riches of mercy and grace stand revealed! –
and then, as our thoughtful and thankful response,
the whole of our lives to the Lord let us yield.

2 Corinthians 9:15; Isaiah 9:6; John 3:16; Romans 8:32;
2 Corinthians 8:9; Philippians 2:7-11; Romans 12:1
Subject Index: B4, F4, H4
11 11 11 11
Suggested Tunes: *Normandy; Montgomery*
See also Appendix A

42

God Has Promised

1 God has promised many things –
treasures from a heavenly store;
now in Christ the echo sounds:
'Yes' to all he said before.
　Think of how he gave his Son –
　such a precious gift indeed!
　How will he not also give
　all that we could ever need?

2 Faith unlocks the power of God
in the face of doubt and fear;
access to his throne is ours –
what can stop us drawing near?
　God has pledged to hear our prayers
　when we ask in Jesus' name,
　so we come with eager hearts
　and his promise boldly claim.

3 Faith enjoys the peace of God –
freedom from anxiety!
What can earthly riches give?
Christ is our security!
　Faith will therefore never cling
　to the wealth we now possess,
　but will find the better way –
　giving freely, keeping less.

4 God has promised many things –
treasures from a heavenly store;
now in Christ the echo sounds:
'Yes' to all he said before.
　So we raise a loud 'Amen!'
　as we make his word our own
　and, with faith to guide our lives,
　make his promised riches known.

2 Corinthians 1:20; Romans 8:32; Ephesians 3:12;
John 14:13-14; Philippians 4:6, 7, 19; Luke 6:38
Subject Index: A4, G3, H6
7 7 7 7 D
Suggested Tunes: *Calon Lân; Aberystwyth; Little Heath*

Good to All His People

God is good to all his people
so with joy we sing and shout:
God is good, without a doubt!

1 In a world of shady dealing,

2 If our anger makes us utter

3 When we see from his perspective

4 Since the Lord is ours for ever,
What in heaven could we desire?
And when mortal powers are failing,
God remains our strength and song,

5 As we follow where he leads us,

Psalm 73
Subject Index: A3, F1, J2
8 77 D refrain 8 77
Suggested Tune: *Wootton Bassett*

Constantly with Us

1 God is our refuge, God is our strength –
  in our distress his presence is near;
  so though the earth quake under our feet,
  safe is his keeping, what shall we fear?

  Constantly with us, faithful and strong –
  God is our shield, our hope and our song.
  Be still and know that he is the Lord,
  ever revered and ever adored!

2 There is a city founded by God,
  filled with his glory, held in his care;
  nations may fall and kingdoms collapse –
  still it remains, that city we share:

3 Come, see his works, his marvellous deeds,
  bringing to nought the power of the sword.
  He is exalted over the earth –
  humbly confess that he is the Lord:

Psalm 46
Subject Index: A4, F1, I1
9 9 9 9 refrain 99 99
Suggested Tune: *Blessed Assurance*

God of Our Salvation

1 God of our salvation,
   how you make us strong;
   how your gifts of joy and comfort
   stir our hearts to song!
   By your loving-kindness
   we are freed from fear,
   drawing from your wells of mercy
   water pure and clear.

2 In our celebrations
   we exalt your name,
   making known to every people
   your unending fame.
   In your holy presence
   we rejoice and sing,
   praising you for all your wonders,
   God our mighty King!

Isaiah 12
Subject Index: A4, F2, H7
6 5 8 5 D
Suggested Tune: *Swahili* (adapted slightly)

Bread of Contentment

1 God our provider,
   rich beyond measure,
   teach us to treasure
      all that is pure:
   keep us from craving
   trinkets that perish
   so that we cherish
      things that endure.

2 Guard us from riches
   if they would harm us –
   things that could charm us,
      lead us astray.
   Spare us from begging,
   needing to borrow;
   bread for tomorrow
      grant us today.

3 May we discover
   your way of living,
   joyfully giving
      plenty, and more;
   Bread of contentment,
   Lord everlasting:
   feasting or fasting,
      you we adore!

1 Timothy 6:7-8; Proverbs 30:8-9; 2 Corinthians 8:2;
Philippians 4:12
Subject Index: F5, H6
5 55 4 D
Suggested Tune: *Bunessan*

Fruit of Goodness

1 God to whom all praise belongs,
God of excellence untold,
you declare that what is pure
has a greater worth than gold:
may the treasures you reveal
set my heart and mind aglow –
as your Spirit works in me
may the fruit of goodness grow.

2 God whose holy call I hear,
God whose words and ways are true,
may complete integrity
be the mark of all I do:
what can counter evil's guile
more than love's sincerity?
May the fruit of goodness grow
as your Spirit works in me.

3 God whose grace is mine to share,
God whose promise I believe,
all the fullness of your life
I am eager to receive.
Freed from sin's oppressive grasp,
more of you I long to know –
as your Spirit works in me
may the fruit of goodness grow.

4 God whose goodness never ends,
let my heart be yours alone;
tune my mind to think your thoughts,
mould my will to match your own;
let me show your righteousness
with untarnished clarity –
may the fruit of goodness grow
as your Spirit works in me.

Philippians 4:8; Galatians 5:22; Romans 12:21; 2 Peter 1:4-5;
Romans 12:2
Subject Index: C, F5, H4
7 7 7 7 D
Suggested Tunes: *Salzburg; Aberystwyth*
See also Appendix B

God, Forever

1 God, to whom the past lies open
  like the pages of a book,
  Lord of countless generations,
  in our age to you we look.
      Through your Son you spoke and called us,
      saved and kept us to this hour –
      gladly we exalt our Saviour,
      Christ, the living Word of power.

2 God, forever present with us,
  nearer than the breath of life,
  Lord of every situation,
  close to us in joy or strife –
      how we need your promised Spirit:
      send the holy flame, we pray!
      Come, renew, refine, inspire us –
      fill our lives afresh, today!

3 God with whom we face the future,
  God our hope, come good or ill,
  we rejoice to know that nothing
  undermines your perfect will.
      Guide us through our earthly journey,
      be our strength, our shield, our light,
      till at last we stand before you –
      till your splendour floods our sight.

Subject Index: A2, H4, I2
8 7 8 7 D
Suggested Tunes: *Austria; Blaenwern*

People of God

1 Hear the good news of the kingdom of God –
comforting words that are challenging too:
if in your spirit you feel you are poor
know that his kingdom is given to you.
If you are mourning, he promises grace,
tenderly healing the pain you have known;
and he declares to the gentle and meek:
you will inherit the earth as your own.

2 Blessed the people who hunger and thirst,
who are determined to follow God's will:
this is the thirst he is certain to quench,
these are the people he promised to fill.
If you show mercy wherever you go
you will find mercy is given to you,
and if your heart is a heart that is pure
you will see God in his purity, too.

3 Those of you striving to bring about peace –
children of God is the name you will bear;
if you are hated for holiness' sake,
then in the kingdom of heaven you share.
You can rejoice if you suffer abuse,
even face death on account of your Lord;
this is the way that the prophets once walked
and you are sure to receive a reward.

4 People of God, you are called to be salt,
stemming the spread of corruption on earth:
but if the salt slips away from your lives
how can you savour, and what are you worth?
Yet you can further the honour of God –
be an example of how to do right:
never be frightened to shine for the truth –
people of God, you are called to be light.

Matthew 5:3-16
Subject Index: B3, H6, J1
10 10 10 10 D
Suggested Tunes: *Hale Bank; Slane**

Emmanuel Means

1 He came to earth in poverty,
a child uniquely holy,
forsaking heaven's majesty
to live among the lowly:

Emmanuel means God has come,
a child of human birth –
and here with us he made his home,
the Son of God on earth.

2 A servant toiling with his hands,
his sovereignty concealing,
our daily lives he understands
with perfect fellow-feeling:

3 In meek obedience stooping down
to taste humiliation,
he freely took a thorny crown
for reconciliation:

4 Emmanuel! Our God is near,
our every sorrow sharing:
he knows our feelings – he is here,
our human frailty bearing:

Subject Index: B2, I1
8 7 8 7 refrain 8 6 8 6
Suggested Tune: *Ach Gott und Herr* (verses) and *Walsall* (refrain)

His Promise Is Sure

1 He has chosen and called us to make us his own;
   we are loved by a Father who made himself known;
   clothed in mercy and peace, and a love without end,
   we are safe in Christ Jesus, our master and friend.

2 He is able to hold us and keep us secure,
   for his purpose is certain, his promise is sure;
   and with holy rejoicing because of his grace
   we shall bask in the glorious light of his face.

3 To the God who has saved us, our voices we raise:
   his unlimited splendour is worthy of praise!
   May he always be worshipped and ever adored
   through his Son, Jesus Christ, our Redeemer and Lord.

Jude 1-2, 24-25
Subject Index: A4, H2, I2
12 12 12 12
Suggested Tune: *Stowey*

Here Is the Lamp

1 Here is the route laid out for us to follow:
   your word reveals the path we ought to tread.
   You teach us how to walk and run in freedom
   when by the truth we let ourselves be led –
       so now we pledge to turn our backs on falsehood,
       and to be guided by your law instead.

2 Here is the spring which offers real refreshment
   to weary hearts, worn down by endless strain:
   within your word we find such inspiration,
   and ample strength to bear our deepest pain.
       Lord, in our lives renew your gracious promise
       and speak the word which makes us strong again.

3 Here is the lamp by whose illumination
   your holy ways lie open to our sight;
   here are the keys of knowledge and discernment:
   through your commands you show us what is right;
       so, Lord, behind the searching beam of Scripture
       we look for you, the Source of perfect light.

Psalm 119 – selected themes
Subject Index: E, F1, H6
11 10 11 10 11 10
Suggested Tune: *Finlandia*

He Spoke

1 He spoke at the beginning,
   and heaven and earth were made –
   in all creation's marvels
   God's splendour is displayed!
   To show his power and goodness
   was his eternal plan –
   his works have borne his hallmark
   since time itself began.

2 He gave his Law to Israel
   to regulate their ways,
   to teach them how to prosper
   through long and fruitful days;
   and then, when his commandments
   were treated with disdain
   he urged them, through his prophets,
   to stop and think again.

3 He spoke to us in Jesus,
   the true, incarnate Word:
   in human speech and language
   the voice of God was heard!
   Christ died, and rose, and brings us
   the truth which sets us free;
   in him we find the pattern
   for all that we should be.

4 His Spirit still is speaking,
   proclaiming what is true:
   in prophecy and preaching
   a message ever new.
   Lord, make our hearts responsive
   to all you want to say:
   your word is life! We need it –
   so speak to us today!

Subject Index: D, E, I2
7 6 7 6 D
Suggested Tunes: *Aurelia; Morning Light*

54

One Who Intercedes

1 Holy Spirit, will you be
   one who intercedes for me?
   When I wonder what to pray,
   how to phrase the words I say,
   come in might and majesty –
   help me in my frailty.

2 Holy Spirit, will you be
   one who intercedes through me?
   When I lack the words to tell
   what my feelings say too well
   speak through every sigh and groan
   making my emotions known.

3 Holy Spirit, will you be
   one who intercedes with me?
   Come, and search my heart and mind,
   my desires and motives find;
   take my deepest thoughts and cares,
   turn them into fervent prayers.

4 Holy Spirit, you will be
   one who intercedes for me!
   You alone can understand
   what the mind of God has planned –
   and within his will you lead
   all for whom you intercede.

Romans 8:26-27
Subject Index: C, F5, H3
77 77 77
Suggested Tunes: *Arfon; Petra*
See also Appendixes A, B

Eternal Treasure

1 Holy Weaver, may we watch you
   guiding life's complexity?
From the threads of joy and sadness,
deftly twining pain and gladness,
you create a single hanging –
   one eternal tapestry.

2 We will listen, truthful Poet –
   listen to your words of grace:
human cries of faith and passion,
grief and hope, you take and fashion
in the saga, yet unfolding,
   of your dealings with our race.

3 Skilful Artist, how we trust you,
   place our hope in you alone:
on a canvas stained with sorrow
you can paint a bright tomorrow
and, with unimagined colours,
   make your sovereign purpose known.

4 We adore you, mighty Goldsmith:
   all to you we gladly yield!
Jeweller in eternal treasure,
for your good and holy pleasure
take our lives, refine and shape us
   till your glory is revealed.

Subject Index: A1, F5, H4
8 7 88 8 7
Suggested Tune: *Edwen*

How Could You

1 How could you leave the splendour
  of undiminished light
  to share a world of shabbiness,
  beset by moral night?
  　　And yet how could you show us
  　　the depths that love will plumb,
  　　or teach us all that life can be,
  　　had you not dared to come?

2 How could you bear the anguish,
  that rift no words can mend –
  betrayal at the hands of one
  you trusted as a friend?
  　　And yet your grief reminds us,
  　　when life is at its worst,
  　　however great our pain may seem
  　　you felt such torment first.

3 How could you find the courage
  to face impending death
  forgiving those whose cruelty
  deprived you of your breath?
  　　And yet, how could you save us
  　　from full and final loss?
  　　The only way to rescue us
  　　meant dying on that cross!

4 How could we ever thank you
  for love so vast and free,
  for mercy which enables us
  to live eternally?
  　　An unsurpassed example,
  　　a debt we cannot pay –
  　　Lord, these evoke our glad response:
  　　to follow and obey.

John 17:5; 1 Timothy 6:16; John 3:19; 1 John 4:9; John 10:10; Matthew 26:21, 49-50; Mark 14:18, 45; Luke 22:22; Psalm 41:9; John 13:18, 21; Luke 23:34; Matthew 26:42; Ephesians 3:18, 2:4-5; 1 Peter 2:21
Subject Index: B4, G2, I2
7 6 8 6 D
Suggested Tune: *Llangloffan*

No Peril We Encounter

1 However great the treasures life affords
    in status or prosperity,
their transitory nature stands exposed:
    they offer scant security.

2 We trust the Lord whose all-creating word
    gave rise to wonders still unknown –
who holds unnumbered stars within his hand
    yet loves to make our hearts his own.

3 Although we may be faced with many trials
    and dangers often close at hand,
no peril we encounter has the power
    to undermine what God has planned.

4 And so, in spite of all the grievous wounds
    which mar a world whose pain we share,
we sense the details of our daily lives
    are held within God's watchful care.

Subject Index: H2, J2
10 8 10 8
See also Appendix A

How Good

1 How good it is to give you thanks:
  we honour you, our mighty King!
  Your endless love, your constant care
  inspire the praise we gladly bring
      in word and music, day and night:
      to worship you is our delight.

2 How glad you make us by your deeds!
  Your thoughts are deep, beyond compare!
  The greatness of your wonders, Lord,
  it is our pleasure to declare;
      to those who place their trust in you
      your glory shines through all you do.

3 How many fail to grasp the truth,
  or hear your voice but turn away;
  they flourish now, but disregard
  the prospect of a judgement day
      when righteousness and mercy meet
      and signal evil's full defeat.

4 And yet how gracious is your call,
  for you address us now as friends
  and guide our lives on fruitful paths
  until, at length, our journey ends:
      Lord God, how matchless are your ways!
      How right it is to sing your praise!

Psalm 92
Subject Index: A3, F1, I2
8 8 8 8 88
Suggested Tune: *St Catherine (Tynemouth)*

Eagles' Wings

1 How good it is to trust in you,
   the mighty King of kings;
   how sheltered is the hiding-place
   we find beneath your wings.

2 No better refuge could we reach –
   protection here is sure!
   However fierce the storms of life,
   with you we are secure.

3 Your presence stills our troubled hearts;
   our doubts and fears decrease –
   in Christ you give us lasting joy
   and all-pervading peace.

4 You see our needs before we ask;
   you hear our every cry;
   and on your utter faithfulness
   we know we can rely.

5 Within the haven of your love
   our strength is forged anew,
   enabling us to rise and soar
   on eagles' wings with you!

Subject Index: F5, G1, H2
8 6 8 6 (CM)
Suggested Tune: *Belmont*

To You Alone

1 How privileged we are,
  that we are called to bring
  our offerings and gifts to you,
  our Sovereign Lord and King!

2 It humbles us to see
  the riches you provide:
  to everyone who seeks your help
  your hand is open wide.

3 What joys you pour on those
  who give with pure delight –
  for all who share with cheerful hearts
  are precious in your sight.

4 Lord, as we bring our gifts
  this longing we express:
  that we may serve you faithfully
  with all that we possess.

5 Within this broken world
  so many needs arise;
  Lord, may our use of wealth become
  creative, bold and wise.

6 So may we worship you
  with everything we own,
  for all we have and give and are
  belong to you alone.

Subject Index: F4, H4, J2
6 6 8 6 (SM)
Suggested Tunes: *Carlisle; Trentham*

Living Sacrifice

1 How rich and deep God's judgements are,
    his knowledge, how profound!
Who understands the path he takes?
    His wisdom, who can sound?
If we should try to guide his thoughts
    no counsel could we find
to offer the all-seeing One
    who forms both heart and mind.

2 And who can give him anything
    which he must then repay,
or charge a debt to his account
    against the judgement day?
Eternal glory and renown
    shall evermore be his –
the Source of all created things,
    the End of all that is!

3 And yet our living sacrifice
    this awesome God desires:
our mortal bodies, yielded up,
    to serve as he requires!
Such giving is a sacred act,
    such worship, pure and right:
the best response of thankful hearts,
    and pleasing in his sight.

4 Then by his all-surpassing power
    our minds he will transform
to see this world's ungodly ways
    no longer as the norm:
for hearts and lives renewed by grace
    at last can truly learn
God's good and pleasing will to prove,
    his judgements to discern.

Romans 11:33-12:2
Subject Index: A4, F2, H4
8 6 8 6 D (DCM)
Suggested Tunes: *Kingsfold; Selfless Love*

The Summons

1   How urgent is the summons
      addressed to us by name:
your holy call is life and death,
      an all-embracing claim;
      and yet our hearts are tepid –
      how slowly we obey
the voice which bids us take the cross
      and follow day by day.

2   From you and from each other
      our flaws we try to hide –
release us from this tyranny
      of self-deceiving pride.
      How seldom are we willing
      to stand for what is right –
renew our vision, purge our fears,
      and nerve us for the fight!

3   Forgive the small ambitions
      which often tie us down,
enticing us to idolise
      achievement or renown;
      seduced by creature-comforts,
      allured by worldly gain,
we need your word to turn our thoughts
      to treasures which remain.

4   From activism spare us –
      how much we try to do!
We struggle to retain control
      instead of trusting you.
      Lord, pardon our reliance
      on energy and skill;
may we be found with servant hearts,
      content to do your will.

Subject Index: F5, H4, I4
7 6 8 6 D
Suggested Tunes: *Llangloffan; St Margaret*

I Bow

I bow before the God of matchless care;
I bow in awe of One I know is always there –
who holds the universe he made entirely in his hand,
but speaks so simply that a little child may understand;
I see the light of welcome in his face;
I dare to call him Father, for he clothes me in his grace –
oh the wonder of his mercy! I can never fathom how
he loves me, and so before his throne I bow.

Subject Index: A1, F2, H2
10 12 14 14 10 14 15 11

I Choose

1 I choose to set my thoughts the way
   the Spirit tells me to:
   to let his life within my mind
   control me through and through,
   control me through and through.

2 I choose to turn my thoughts away
   from sin and its desires –
   from things which neither honour God
   nor do what he requires,
   nor do what he requires.

3 I choose to take the Spirit's gift,
   the pathway of release:
   for all who let him rule their minds
   discover life and peace,
   discover life and peace.

4 Lord, may your Spirit give to me
   new life in place of old –
   by fallen values let my thoughts
   no longer be controlled,
   no longer be controlled.

5 Praise God – where Christ is named as Lord
   his Spirit can be found –
   and where the Spirit makes his home,
   his power and life abound,
   his power and life abound.

Romans 8:5-9
Subject Index: C, F5, H6
8 6 8 6 (CM) Extended
Suggested Tune: *St Magnus* (last line not repeated)
See also Appendix B

Out of the Grasp of Death

1 I love you, Lord, for you answered me
    when I was close to despair:
I called for help in a time of strife,
when fears of death overwhelmed my life –
    and found that you heard my prayer.

2 To those who know of your righteousness,
    your gracious promise is clear:
for your compassion is great indeed,
and your assurance is all I need
    to deal with my anxious fear.

3 Lord, you delivered my soul from death,
    my life from stumbling and tears;
though few acknowledge your ways are true,
my pledge remains: I shall walk with you
    the rest of my earthly years.

4 For all the love you have shown to me
    my heartfelt thanks I will bring:
I stand, a debtor to boundless grace
as with your people I take my place,
    confessing you Lord and King.

5 How great the freedom your service gives –
    no better life could there be! –
till in the hour of my final breath
you lead me out of the grasp of death
    to serve you eternally.

Psalm 116
Subject Index: A4, F1, H6
9 7 99 7
Suggested Tune: *Aigburth Vale*

Like Jesus

1 In all things God is working out
   his good, eternal plan:
the Father's sovereign hand we find
retaining full control behind
all circumstances, harsh or kind,
   since time itself began.

2 He fashions for our benefit
   the worlds of time and space:
he knew our names from long ago,
and planned within our lives to show
how much he offers those who know
   the breadth and depth of grace.

3 Our hope is Christ, the eldest son
   of one great family:
for those God chose, he called aside,
and those he called, he justified
and destined to be glorified –
   like Jesus we shall be!

Romans 8:28-30
Subject Index: G2, I3, J2
8 6 888 6
Suggested Tune: *Revelation*
See also Appendixes A, B

Heal Our Nation

1 In an age of twisted values
     we have lost the truth we need;
in sophisticated language
     we have justified our greed;
by our struggle for possessions
     we have robbed the poor and weak –
hear our cry and heal our nation:
     your forgiveness, Lord, we seek.

2 We have built discrimination
     on our prejudice and fear;
hatred swiftly turns to cruelty
     if we hold resentments dear.
For communities divided
     by the walls of class and race
hear our cry and heal our nation:
     show us, Lord, your love and grace.

3 When our families are broken;
     when our homes are full of strife;
when our children are bewildered,
     when they lose their way in life;
when we fail to give the aged
     all the care we know we should –
hear our cry and heal our nation
     with your tender fatherhood.

4 We who hear your word so often
     choose so rarely to obey;
turn us from our wilful blindness,
     give us truth to light our way.
In the power of your Spirit
     come to cleanse us, make us new:
hear our cry and heal our nation
     till our nation honours you.

Subject Index: F5, G2, H3
8 7 8 7 D
Suggested Tunes: *Bethany; Kilve*

Trustworthy and True

1 Incarnate Word, you spoke the truth
 to all whose hearts were tuned to hear;
 where falsehood and injustice lurk
 we find your voice still crystal-clear;
  and now your Spirit lives in us,
  confirming what our lips confess:
  Lord Jesus, may our words resound
  with echoes of your faithfulness.

2 You showed the Father's steadfast love –
 eternal care, yet ever new! –
 and said the key to knowing God
 is simply that we follow you.
  Directed by your Spirit's touch,
  we choose your lifestyle as our own,
  and ask that through our faithfulness
  your love will be more widely known.

3 So may we use the gifts you give
 with self-effacing diligence
 to bear the lasting fruit you want,
 our love shown by obedience.
  With your example prompting us,
  may we prove trustworthy and true –
  Lord, by consistent faithfulness
  may we delight and honour you!

Subject Index: B3, G1, H7
8 8 8 8 D
Suggested Tune: *Addison's (London)*
See also Appendix B

Present Sufferings

1 In the face of present sufferings,
   Christians, let us not forget:
   there are greater glories coming
   than we have envisaged yet!
   All creation waits, expectant,
   till God's handiwork is known:
   till the children of his promise
   to a watching world are shown.

2 Countless solar systems wrestle
   with frustration and decay
   till the climax of the ages,
   when their chains are swept away.
   Now, we sense the pains of childbirth
   which the cosmos has to bear;
   then, the freedom we inherit
   all the universe will share.

3 We who taste the Spirit's firstfruits
   still are groaning inwardly,
   yearning for our full redemption,
   for our bodies' liberty.
   To be God's perfected children
   is the hope by which we live;
   patience, brother, sister, patience:
   what he promised, God will give.

Romans 8:18-25
Subject Index: H1, I2, J4
8 7 8 7 D
Suggested Tunes: *Bolsterstone; Ebenezer (Ton-y-Botel)*
See also Appendix B

Newness

1 In the garden Mary lingers,
    broken and forlorn,
    then an unexpected greeting
    names her in the dawn:
    so she meets her risen Saviour
    on the resurrection morn.

2 Evening journey: two disciples,
    grieving for the dead,
    find a stranger walks beside them,
    cheers their hearts instead –
    finally they recognise him
    as he breaks and shares the bread.

3 Ten distraught, confused apostles
    hide away in fear;
    rumours that the grave is empty
    they are shocked to hear –
    yet when Jesus stands among them
    dread and sorrow disappear.

4 Fishermen who toiled for nothing
    on the lake all night
    hear the sound of Jesus' welcome
    in the morning light:
    in the friendship shared at breakfast
    old mistakes are lost to sight.

5 Every day a fresh beginning –
    newness, come what may!
    In the most unlikely places
    Jesus reigns today;
    from the past to new horizons
    Christ our Saviour leads the way.

Subject Index: B5, I1, J1
8 5 8 5 8 7
Suggested Tune: *Angel Voices*

The Sound of Crying

1 In the night, the sound of crying –
whimpers from a babe so small:
angels hail the newborn infant
in that dingy cattle-stall.

2 In the night, the sound of crying –
Mary journeys on with tears,
further from the home she treasures,
onward to uncertain years.

3 In the night, the sound of crying –
fury nothing can assuage!
Schemes of pointless, brutal murder
spring from Herod's jealous rage.

4 In the night, the sound of crying –
agonies beyond belief!
Soldiers searching, children slaughtered –
parents overwhelmed with grief.

5 In the night, the sound of crying –
cries of faith, though hope looks vain;
cries of joy, for Christ has conquered,
and, with justice, comes to reign.

Subject Index: B2, J3
8 7 8 7
Suggested Tunes: *St Andrew; Sussex*

Jesus Stands

1 Jesus stands among the children
smeared with others' guilt at birth –
haunted by unspoken questions,
made to feel devoid of worth.
Refugees from threat or danger,
far from home through troubled years:
Jesus senses all their turmoil –
parents' anguish, children's fears.

2 Jesus stands with those rejected
by their nearest flesh and blood,
feeling sorrow with the lonely,
shunned, and seldom understood.
Jesus walks among the homeless,
where the street becomes a bed –
finding, far from heaven's splendour,
nowhere else to lay his head.

3 Jesus stands where justice falters,
where the truth is bought and sold:
well he knows the bitter poison
of a trust betrayed for gold.
Lies and groundless accusations;
torture dealt by callous hands;
execution, slow and painful –
each of these he understands.

4 Jesus bids us stand beside him –
Man of sorrows, Lord of all! –
as with wounded hands he offers
grace and strength to those who fall.
He transforms our path of suffering,
brings us newness by his pain;
in the help we give to others
we begin to share his reign.

Subject Index: B2, G1, J1
8 7 8 7 D
Suggested Tune: *Bethany*

Where You Lead Us

1 Jesus, we have heard your Spirit
saying we belong to you,
showing us our need for mercy,
focusing our hopes anew;
you have won our hearts' devotion,
now we feel your guiding hand:
where you lead us, we will follow
on the paths your love has planned.

2 As a chosen, pilgrim people
we are learning day by day
what it means to be disciples,
to believe and to obey.
Word and table show your purpose;
hearts and lives we gladly bring –
where you lead us, we will follow,
suffering Saviour, risen King.

3 How we yearn that every people
should exalt your matchless name,
yet so often this world's systems
countermand your regal claim.
If we stand for truth and justice
we, like you, may suffer loss;
where you lead us, we will follow –
give us grace to bear our cross.

4 So we journey on together,
keen to make our calling sure:
through our joys, our fears, our crises,
may our faith be made mature.
Jesus, hope of hearts and nations,
sovereign Lord of time and space,
where you lead us, we will follow
till we see you face to face.

Subject Index: H6, I2, J1
8 7 8 7 D
Suggested Tune: *Ode to Joy*

To Be Meek

1 Jesus, you have shown us how
to be humble, to be meek –
always tender, always kind,
neither compromised nor weak –
for your life and death alike
show the truth of all you spoke;
still, today, we hear your voice,
calling us to bear your yoke.

2 In our hearts we crown you King,
on our lips your name is heard,
and we willingly submit
to the teaching of your word –
so a trusted friend's rebuke
is a welcome blow indeed
when it leads us to the truth
and the discipline we need.

3 Let humility and grace
be the clothing that we wear
as in genuine concern
one another's loads we bear.
May we love, and not condemn,
those who stumble, slip or fall;
let us help them once again
to receive your gracious call.

4 Though regarded by this world
with suspicion or disdain
still the meek enjoy your pledge:
all this earth they will obtain!
For the treasure in their hearts
has a value yet untold –
give us, Lord, that precious grace
which surpasses finest gold.

Matthew 11:29; 1 Peter 3:15; James 1:21; Psalm 141:5;
Colossians 3:12; Galatians 6:1; Matthew 5:5; 1 Peter 3:4
Subject Index: B3, F5, H6
7 7 7 7 D
Suggested Tunes: *St Edmund; Salzburg*
See also Appendix B

Let Hymns of Joyful Praise

1 Let hymns of joyful praise abound
and countless human voices sound;
let songs of worship echo round,
proclaiming that the King is crowned!

2 Bring skilful words and melody,
bring rhythm, too, and harmony
to celebrate in rhapsody
the Lord of endless majesty.

3 The Lamb who once was crucified
is seated at his Father's side;
his name is honoured far and wide –
our voices join the swelling tide.

4 Our worship we delight to bring,
for he has given everything –
and evermore the cry shall ring
that Jesus Christ is Lord and King!

Subject Index: B6, F3, J4
8888 (LM)
Suggested Tunes: *Agincourt; Bow Brickhill*
See also Appendix A

Let Love Be Found

1 Let love be found among us –
the gift of God it is,
the hallmark of his children,
the sign that we are his.
We claim that God has called us –
no idle boast or fraud
if love directs our actions
and proves we know the Lord!

2 The reason God has loved us
is simply sovereign choice –
our love is but an echo
to his resounding voice:
for God is love, and showed it
by giving us his Son:
through him our past is pardoned –
a new life has begun.

3 How deeply God has loved us,
accepting us as friends –
so let us show each other
this love which never ends:
for though we cannot find him
with sight or touch or sound,
yet God himself is present
where love is truly found.

1 John 4:7-12
Subject Index: G1, H6, I3
7 6 7 6 D
Suggested Tunes: *Wolvercote; Penlan; Nettleton*
See also Appendixes A, B

Nothing but the Cross

Let me boast in nothing but the cross
where the Lord was crucified;
I will place my pride in nothing else
but the cross where Jesus died.

1 On the cross he took what I deserved,
   gave his life to set me free:
   there he bore the judgement on my sin,
   made himself accursed for me.
   When I failed to live by God's commands
   Jesus suffered in my place;
   here I find the pardon which removes
   both my guilt and my disgrace:

2 But the cross spells death for me as well:
   I am crucified with Christ –
   everything I used to be has died
   since my Lord was sacrificed.
   Now the key to life is faith in him,
   since his promise I believe;
   his unending resurrection life
   is the gift I now receive:

3 So this world and I have parted now –
   very different paths we take! –
   all the worthless idols of this age
   Christ commands me to forsake.
   Earthly fame and riches cannot last,
   neither will they satisfy;
   at my Saviour's cross I take my stand,
   and for him I live or die:

Galatians 3:13, 2:20, 6:14
Subject Index: B4, G3, H4
9 7 9 7 D refrain 9 7 9 7

Let Us Exalt

1 Let us exalt our King,
   offer our finest praise;
daily, and evermore,
   let us applaud his ways!
How right that he should be adored –
our great, unfathomable Lord.

2 Tell of his majesty,
   splendours of dazzling light;
speak of the awesome power
   shown in his acts of might!
As on these things we meditate,
how can we help but celebrate?

3 Under his gracious reign
   mercy will never fail;
anger is seldom found,
   kindness and love prevail:
his kingdom ever will endure,
a realm eternally secure.

4 Promises made – and kept;
   love which embraces all;
strength for the weary heart,
   courage for those who fall –
our God provides what each requires;
he loves to meet our hearts' desires.

5 Let us exalt our King,
   serve him in godly fear –
trusting his saving power,
   conscious that he is near.
How right it is to spread his fame!
Let every being praise his name!

Psalm 145
Subject Index: A4, F1, H7
6 6 6 6 88
Suggested Tune: *Little Cornard*

In His Risen Life

1 Let us lift our hearts in praise:
  Christ our King is on his throne!
  Let us turn our thoughts to him –
  we are his and his alone.
  In his risen life we share
  since with him we also died;
  all his joy and peace are ours
  when his Spirit is our guide.

2 Dead to sin, alive to God –
  such a liberty we find!
  All this world's ungodly ways
  we are glad to leave behind.
  From the snare of selfishness
  God our Father set us free –
  rescued by the death of Christ,
  we are called to purity.

3 If we feel temptation's lure,
  Jesus knows and understands;
  if we find our load too great
  we can place it in his hands.
  When we come to him for help
  he will never hide his face,
  but will give us all we need:
  ample strength, abundant grace.

4 So with glad and thankful hearts
  let us aim to please the Lord,
  knowing all we do for him
  he has promised to reward.
  Let us live as Jesus did,
  serving him through all our days,
  blending every word and deed
  in a lifelong hymn of praise.

Colossians 3:1-3; Romans 8:6, 6:2; Titus 2:12-14; Hebrews 2:18;
1 Peter 5:7; Hebrews 4:14-16; Colossians 3:17, 23-24;
2 Corinthians 5:9; Ephesians 5:10; 1 John 2:5-6
Subject Index: B6, H6, I2
7 7 7 7 D
Suggested Tune: *St George's Windsor*

Hopes of Glory

1 Let us rejoice: God's gift to us is peace!
   Here is the calm which bids our strivings cease,
   for God's acceptance brings a true release:
      alleluia!

2 We can be strong, for now we stand by grace,
   held in his loving, fatherly embrace;
   his care remains, whatever trials we face:
      alleluia!

3 We trust in God, and shall not be dismayed,
   nor find our hopes of glory are betrayed,
   for all his splendour we shall see displayed:
      alleluia!

4 And come what may, we never need despair –
   God is at work through all the griefs we bear,
   that in the end his likeness we may share:
      alleluia!

5 Deep in our hearts the love of God is found;
   his precious gifts of life and joy abound –
   so let our finest songs of praise resound:
      alleluia!

Romans 5:1-5
Subject Index: F3, G2, H2
10 10 10 4
Suggested Tunes: *Engleberg; Sine Nomine*
See also Appendix A

Lift High the Cross

1 Lift high the cross: the sign of God's commitment
  to save a world which turns against the light;
  here Jesus blazed the trail for liberation,
  by love and death disarming evil's might.

2 Lift high the cross: our model for involvement
  within the structures of this present age –
  for we are called to follow Christ's agenda,
  and in the fight for justice to engage.

3 Lift high the cross – and let it be our standard,
  the word we speak, the challenge we must bring,
  and in humility confront the cultures
  which will not bow and honour Christ as King.

4 Lift high the cross – the load we carry daily,
  the costly call no Christian may ignore:
  misunderstanding, hatred or rejection –
  we tread the path which Jesus trod before.

5 Lift high the cross: the key to resurrection –
  no harvest comes except from buried seed;
  yet those who face discouragement and sorrow
  find here at last the peace and hope they need.

Subject Index: B4, I4, J1
11 10 11 10
Suggested Tune: *Intercessor*
See also Appendix A

Born to Die

1 Long ago, in a town so obscure,
   born a babe to a mother so poor;
   not a cradle to cushion his head,
   but a stall in a stable his bed;
   see the child as he slumbers, and yet
   hear the truth we must never forget –
   he was born to die:

   Born to walk in the way of the cross,
   born to share in humanity's loss,
   born to pay the incredible price –
   God's only Son was the sacrifice –
   he was born to die.

2 Hear the words of the heavenly throng:
   joyous tidings, their jubilant song.
   Tell the people a Saviour is born,
   thrilling news for a world so forlorn.
   Shepherds hasten, the baby to see;
   what is this special infant to be?
   He was born to die:

3 Men of majesty, travelling far,
   come to Bethlehem, led by a star.
   Precious gold, myrrh and incense they bring
   to present to the newly born King;
   as in homage to Jesus they bow
   do they know what we realise now? –
   He was born to die:

4 Refugees on the run in the night,
   from the anger of Herod their flight.
   Still the world offers Jesus no place –
   and would you turn your back on his face?
   Let the Bethlehem baby come in;
   he was born to release you from sin –
   he was born to die:

Subject Index: B2, G2
99 99 99 5 refrain 99 99 5
Suggested Tune: *Sacrifice*

God Eternal, One, yet Three

1 Long ago the Father's voice
brought the universe to birth –
by his mighty Living Word
he created heaven and earth;
then he gave the gift of life
by the holy Breath he blew!
God eternal, One, yet Three,
all creation's source is you.

2 From before the dawn of time
chosen as the Father's own,
we receive his gift of grace
by the death of Christ alone;
now we feel the Spirit's touch –
power to set our lives ablaze!
God eternal, One, yet Three,
how we love your gracious ways!

3 God our Father makes his home
in each heart which loves the Son;
when we live as Jesus taught,
then the Father's will is done.
We shall know our Lord's commands
as we heed his Spirit's voice –
God eternal, One, yet Three,
glad obedience is our choice.

4 In the temple of the Lord,
Jesus is the cornerstone;
in our lives, both fruit and gifts
make his Spirit's presence known;
so the Church of God is built
to become a holy place:
God eternal, One, yet Three,
let your people grow in grace.

5 Father, we revere your name –
great Creator, sovereign King;
Jesus, Saviour, Son of God,
praise to you we gladly bring;
Holy Spirit, Breath of life,
you we honour and adore;
God eternal, One, yet Three,
be exalted evermore!

Genesis 1:1, 2:7; John 1:2-3; Ephesians 1:4-7, 13; John 14:15, 21, 16:15;
Ephesians 2:21-22; 1 Corinthians 12:3-4; Galatians 5:22
Subject Index: D, F2, I2
7 7 7 7 D
Suggested Tunes: *St Edmund; St George's Windsor*

This Grace of Sharing

1 Long ago you taught your people:
   'Part of what you reap is mine –
   from your cattle, bring the firstborn;
   tithe the crops of field and vine.'
   Though beneath the law's restrictions
   we are not compelled to live,
   as we reap our monthly harvest,
   make us eager, Lord, to give.

2 What a way of life you showed us
   through the Son you gladly gave:
   never snared by earthly treasure,
   buried in a borrowed grave –
   yet to all he freely offered
   riches of the deepest kind:
   let us live with his example
   firmly fixed in heart and mind.

3 In the lifestyle of the Spirit
   giving has a central part;
   teach us, Lord, this grace of sharing
   with a cheerful, loving heart –
   not a tiresome obligation,
   not a barren legal due,
   but an overflow of worship:
   all we have belongs to you!

Subject Index: D, F4, H4
8 7 8 7 D
Suggested Tune: *Ode to Joy*

Great Judge of All

1 Lord, do you see the evil in the world?
  Look how the weak are crushed, the poor oppressed!
  Will you ignore the arrogant and proud,
  scorning the anguish of the dispossessed?
    You are the one who fashions eye and ear:
    great Judge of all, you surely see and hear!

2 You discipline the nations of the earth;
  in all your dealings you are just and fair.
  Those whom you call your people, you sustain,
  making them stronger by the griefs they bear.
    Happy are all who learn to understand
    the love revealed by your correcting hand.

3 Though we have often felt that all was lost
  your faithful care has always brought us through;
  still when the threat of evil is so real,
  strong is our refuge as we trust in you.
    On your unfailing promise we depend:
    your righteous love will triumph in the end!

Psalm 94
Subject Index: A3, F1, G3, J2
10 10 10 10 10 10
Suggested Tune: *Song 1*

Great King of the Ages

1 Lord God Almighty, our praises we bring:
  your name is exalted, your honours we sing –
    your splendour through age after age is revealed,
    your people's salvation, our strength and our shield.

2 Marvellous things beyond number you do;
  your justice is flawless, your judgements are true.
    Let all of the nations confess you as Lord,
    great King of the ages, revered and adored.

3 No one is like you, the First and the Last,
  in glory unrivalled, in might unsurpassed.
    On righteousness founded, your throne is secure –
    whoever your foes are, your triumph is sure.

4 You will provide us with all that we need:
  so, gladly, we follow wherever you lead,
    until in your presence in heaven we stand,
    enjoying the fulness of all you have planned.

5 Marvellous things beyond number you do;
  your justice is flawless, your judgements are true.
    We give you our worship, for you are our Lord,
    great King of the ages, revered and adored!

Exodus 15:1-18; Revelation 15:3-4
Subject Index: A3, F3, J4
10 11 11 11
Suggested Tune: *Slane*

I Gladly Trust

1 Lord, I gladly trust in you:
  let me not be put to shame.
      As I look towards your throne
      make your gracious promise known:
  God my refuge and my hope,
  your protective care I claim.

2 In your hands I place my past:
  all my sins you know so well.
      Your forgiveness, Lord, I need,
      for my guilt is great indeed;
  even greater is your love –
  mercy more than I can tell.

3 Teach me what is true and good;
  let me hear and understand!
      In the choices I must make
      show my heart the way to take,
  so that I may always tread
  on the path which you have planned.

4 When my troubles multiply
  you alone can bring me through:
      so with all your saints I say,
      'Be my strength and shield today.'
  Since I know you hear my prayer,
  Lord, I gladly trust in you.

Psalm 25
Subject Index: F1, G3, H3
7 7 77 7 7
Suggested Tunes: *Petra; Ratisbon*

The Seeds of Self-Control

1 Lord Jesus, by your mercy
   I stand both free and whole,
   and in my heart discover
   the seeds of self-control.

2 I realise your Spirit
   has made his home in me,
   for holiness reshaping
   my personality.

3 No more need I be driven
   by bodily desires –
   you call me to the passion
   which servant-love inspires.

4 Your Spirit gently nurtures
   the discipline of prayer,
   and kindles my commitment
   to witness and to care.

5 So faith becomes the keynote
   of everything I do,
   and your complete approval
   the prize which I pursue.

6 Lord Jesus, fill my spirit,
   my body and my soul;
   produce in me a harvest
   of godly self-control.

John 8:36; Galatians 5:23; 1 Corinthians 6:19; Romans 12:2, 8:26, 5:5;
2 Corinthians 5:7, 9; 1 Corinthians 9:25
Subject Index: G2, H1
7 6 7 6
Suggested Tune: *St Alphege*
See also Appendix B

More of You

1 Lord Jesus, plant a seed of faith
  and let it grow in me,
  to bear a harvest shown by deeds
  of lasting quality.

2 Grant me a gentle, humble heart
  where love alone holds sway,
  till selfless servanthood becomes
  my habit day by day.

3 Give me a deeper, richer hope,
  a vision sure and clear,
  to strengthen me until the day
  when you at last appear.

4 I have no faith but what you give;
  your love has made me new;
  my hope is found in no one else –
  Lord, give me more of you!

1 Thessalonians 1:3
Subject Index: F5, G3, H6
8 6 8 6 (CM)
Suggested Tunes: *Abridge; Martyrdom*

Lord of Compassion

1 Lord of compassion, gracious and kind,
yours is a love which cares for us all;
Shepherd whose voice was known by your sheep,
still those who listen find that you call.
Hearing that call, we wonder indeed
why should you think us worth such a cost;
yet in our place you willingly died,
spending your life to rescue the lost.

2 Freedom you bring from all that enslaves;
worries you change for treasure untold;
and to the poor you offer a realm
where there are riches finer than gold.
Pardon us, Lord, that deep in our hearts
greed and injustice still we can find;
write on our lives your gracious concern
till we are loving, gentle and kind.

3 Tender your touch to soothe and restore:
healing you bring to body and soul.
Mighty in death, you conquered disease –
risen again, your life makes us whole.
Lord of compassion, right to the cross –
'Here is your son' and 'Father, forgive' –
teach us to walk your way on the earth;
work through us, Lord, as long as we live.

Subject Index: B3, F5, G1
9 9 9 9 D

The Promise

1 Lord, we thank you for the promise
seen in every human birth:
you have planned each new beginning –
who could hope for greater worth?
Hear our prayer for those we cherish:
claim our children as your own –
in the fertile ground of childhood
may eternal seed be sown.

2 Lord, we thank you for the vigour
burning in the years of youth:
strength to face tomorrow's challenge,
zest for life and zeal for truth.
In the choice of friends and partners,
when ideas and values form,
may the message of your kingdom
be the guide, the goal, the norm.

3 Lord, we thank you for the harvest
of the settled, middle years:
times when work and home can prosper,
when life's richest fruit appears;
but when illness, stress and hardship
fill so many days with dread,
may your love renew the vision
of a clearer road ahead.

4 Lord, we thank you for the beauty
of a heart at last mature:
crowned with peace and rich in wisdom,
well-respected and secure;
but to those who face the twilight
frail, bewildered, lacking friends,
Lord, confirm your gracious offer:
perfect life which never ends.

Subject Index: F5, H3, J2
8 7 8 7 D
Suggested Tunes: *Abbot's Leigh; The Promise; Deerhurst*

God of Mercy

1 Lord, we turn to you for mercy:
   may our prayerful words express
   something of our heartfelt sorrow
   for the sins we now confess.

2 We have trusted far too often
   in our human strength and skill;
   we have proudly disregarded
   what we knew to be your will.

3 Yet by your immense compassion
   you invite, accept, restore,
   leading us to greater wholeness
   than we ever knew before.

4 Your forgiveness lifts our burdens,
   setting heart and spirit free
   to fulfil our true potential,
   all that we were meant to be.

5 For you teach a way of wisdom
   we may clearly understand:
   walking with the God of mercy
   step by step, and hand in hand.

Hosea 14
Subject Index: F5, G2, H3
8 7 8 7
Suggested Tunes: *Gott Will's Machen; All for Jesus*

Human Frame

1 Lord, you designed our human frame –
on you our lives depend;
your word can heal our illnesses,
our broken bodies mend:
so hear us as we call for help –
your gracious power extend.

2 We boldly come before your throne
in prayer, as you command,
to ask that those who suffer pain
may feel your gentle hand:
we dare to seek the healing touch
your perfect love has planned.

3 For Jesus, when he walked this earth,
brought wholeness everywhere:
no need too great for him to meet,
no grief too small to share –
in him you have revealed to us
your ever-present care.

4 And if it seems no answers come,
still in that care we rest,
until, refined by discipline,
we prove your ways are best:
so grant us courage to believe
as faith pursues its quest.

5 For Christ has shared our life and death,
our frail mortality:
his resurrection shows us now
what, one day, we shall be –
new bodies and eternal life
remain our destiny!

Subject Index: F5, H3, J2
8 6 8 6 8 6
Suggested Tunes: *All Hallows; Brother James' Air*

May the Grace

1 May the grace of Christ, our Saviour,
   be our guide in all we do,
   for his willing self-abasement
   shows the pathway to pursue;
   as we give to other people
   may he make us rich indeed,
   bringing to our human frailty
   all the strength he knows we need.

2 May the love of God our Father
   clothe and fill us day by day;
   may compassion be our watchword
   and forgiveness chart our way –
   for to holiness he called us,
   to reflect his purity:
   in our actions may his kindness
   be a light for all to see.

3 May the friendship of God's Spirit
   be a joy forever near;
   in our times of doubt and trouble
   may his presence banish fear.
   As his comfort makes us stronger,
   glorious freedom may we know;
   by the life of God he brings us,
   more like Jesus may we grow.

2 Corinthians 13:14, 8:9, 9:6, 12:9; 1 John 4:8; Ephesians 4:32;
1 Peter 1:15; Matthew 5:16; 2 Corinthians 3:17-18, 1:4-5
Subject Index: D, H6, I1
8 7 8 7 D
Suggested Tunes: *In Babilone; Blaenwern*

(This text can also be sung in the second person rather than the first:

> May the grace of Christ, your Saviour,
> be your guide in all you do…

Such usage may be suitable for a commissioning service.)

More than Words

1 More than words can say
   is your love to me,
now and evermore:
   love to set me free
   and to make me whole,
love that fills my heart,
   flooding through my soul
more than words can say.

2 Chosen to be loved,
   I am made anew
by your endless grace;
   called to be like you
   and to make you known,
now and evermore
   I am yours alone –
what a destiny!

3 Lord, you are to me
   more than words can say,
and I worship you;
   God whom I obey
   and whom I adore,
this is my desire:
   now and evermore
may I honour you.

Subject Index: F2, G1, H2
5 5 5 5 D
Suggested Tune: *Longfield*

Kindness

1 My Father, full of endless love,
   compassionate and kind,
   to your unchanging faithfulness
   no limits can I find.

2 In Christ you showed your care for all,
   both crowds and those alone –
   whatever human needs he found,
   he made your kindness known.

3 Now may your Spirit touch my heart
   with love's consuming fire:
   creative, kind and thoughtful deeds
   within my life inspire.

4 With stranger, friend and foe alike
   your kindness I would share;
   this fruit your Spirit nurtures, Lord,
   is one I long to bear.

Subject Index: D, G1, H6
8 6 8 6 (CM)
Suggested Tune: *St Agnes (Dykes)*
See also Appendix B

Footsteps

1 My Lord, you called my name
   before the world began,
   and chose that I should be
   included in your plan.

2 How well you know my heart;
   its hidden depths you see;
   and yet you love me still
   and freely pardon me.

3 You feel my every care,
   each hope and each desire;
   my burdens you relieve,
   new visions you inspire.

4 From long before my birth
   my every path you knew –
   I bless you that you turned
   my footsteps back to you!

Subject Index: F5, G1, H1
6 6 6 6
Suggested Tunes: *Ibstone; Quam Dilecta*

Through and Through

1 My Lord, you have examined me,
  you know me through and through;
  you see my deeds, perceive my thoughts,
  my speech, my motives too.
  You wrap me round on every side;
  on me you place your hand:
  such knowledge is too wonderful
  for me to understand!

2 The presence of your Spirit will
  be with me to the last;
  wherever I decide to go
  your love will hold me fast.
  If I should try to run from you
  I know without a doubt
  no darkness could conceal my path –
  your light would shine me out.

3 You made me in my mother's womb,
  so intricate your ways,
  and even then, before my birth,
  you numbered all my days.
  Before I sleep and as I wake
  I know that you are there:
  how could I ever sound the depths
  of your unfailing care?

4 And yet I find my soul perturbed
  by bitterness and grief,
  for many choose to treat your word
  with scornful unbelief –
  so search me, Lord, and cleanse my heart
  from all that you abhor,
  then teach me how to walk with you
  today and evermore.

Psalm 139
Subject Index: F1, H2
8 6 8 6 D (DCM)
Suggested Tune: *Kingsfold*

No Condemnation

1 No condemnation holds us now
   for Christ has set us free;
   to all who yearn for righteousness
   his death provides the key –
   for where the Spirit sets the pace
   the flesh no longer has a place;
   in Jesus we become, by grace,
   the people we should be.

2 A law of sin, a law of death,
   a consequence of blame:
   our fine ideals slipped away
   and left us only shame.
   God's law we never could fulfil –
   our human weakness failed us still –
   but Jesus did the Father's will
   within a mortal frame.

3 For he became the offering
   which clears our awful debt
   and opens up a way of life
   no more by sin beset;
   so as we follow Christ today
   the call to freedom we obey –
   and where the Spirit leads the way
   the law's demands are met.

Romans 8:1-4
Subject Index: G2, H1, I2
8 6 8 6 888 6
Suggested Tune: *The Staff of Faith*
See also Appendix B

100

All Our Life and Light

1 No other prophet ever spoke
    so clearly to our race;
no bright and shining angel matched
    the glory on his face;
through him the universe was made,
by him our debt for sin was paid –
in Christ, at last, we see in full
    God's splendour and God's grace.

2 Majestic angels swiftly fly
    on wings of wind and flame;
his servants' servants, low they bend
    in honour of his name.
The Father's precious Son is he,
the Lord from all eternity –
yet taking human flesh and blood
    a baby he became.

3 His throne is built on righteousness,
    established firm and sure;
the oil of joy anoints the one
    who values what is pure!
The wonder of the Maker's skill
is seen throughout creation still –
but when this age has run its course
    his kingdom will endure.

4 God's matchless power confirms that Christ
    is all our life and light:
his word proclaims the solemn truth
    dividing wrong from right,
and those who cast that word aside
are lost like driftwood on the tide –
but Jesus reigns eternally
    in majesty and might!

Hebrews 1:1-2:4
Subject Index: B1, E, J2
8 6 8 6 88 8 6
Suggested Tune: *The Staff of Faith*
See also Appendix A

Celebrate the Mighty Triumphs

1 Once so many regulations
kept us from God's holy throne;
Jesus gave his life to save us,
made our sin and guilt his own –
by his death and resurrection
God's forgiveness can be known.

2 From the Fall came devastation –
sickness took a heavy toll;
Jesus brought the Father's power,
healing body, mind and soul;
on the cross he shared our weakness,
suffered there to make us whole.

3 Satan's dark and evil forces
tried to overcome the light;
Jesus challenged their rebellion,
blazed the truth into the night:
when he died he crushed the serpent,
trampled him and won the fight.

4 Over life the fear of dying
cast a shadow of despair;
death is now completely conquered:
resurrection we can share –
Jesus has gone on before us,
homes in heaven to prepare.

5 Celebrate the mighty triumphs
won by Jesus when he died!
Though he bore humiliation
once when he was crucified,
now he reigns, the risen victor,
seated at the Father's side!

Subject Index: B4, F3, H5
8 7 8 7 8 7
Suggested Tune: *Neander*
See also Appendix A

One Man Alone

1 One man, alone, in unremitting darkness,
  knowing his life is soon to reach its end,
  prays for the strength to face the coming moment:
  a traitor's kiss from one he called a friend.

2 One man, alone, he faces his accusers –
  judges who neither care nor understand;
  nothing he says in answer to their questions
  can change a fate he knows has long been planned.

3 Scourging and thorns, then nails and crucifixion:
  who can believe the pain this man must bear?
  Then at the point when evil seems to triumph
  he yields his life to God's unfailing care.

4 One Man alone has drawn the sting of evil –
  he has the right to sit on heaven's throne!
  Yet he is glad to stand with those who suffer:
  so we need never face our trials alone.

Matthew 26:36-39, 48-49, 59-60, 27:26; Mark 3:6, 14:32-36,
44-45, 55, 15:15; Luke 22:41-42, 66-71, 23:33, 46; John 19:16;
1 Corinthians 15:56; Hebrews 1:3, 13:5-6; Acts 18:9; 2 Timothy 4:17
Subject Index: B4, H2
11 10 11 10
Suggested Tune: *O Perfect Love*

Humble Dignity

1 One whose heart is hard as steel
joins the others for the meal;
time for Judas now to choose:
light or darkness, win or lose?
Has it really come to this?
Cold betrayal with a kiss!

2 Simon Peter speaks for all,
swears that he will never fall.
Near the fire, the pressure grows –
three denials – cockerel crows –
wounded love in Jesus' eyes;
Peter hides away, and cries.

3 Sent to Caiaphas the priest
to be judged before the feast:
wildest accusations fly –
'By our law this man should die!' –
yet that law was his, which they
claim to cherish and obey.

4 'What is truth? Are you a king?'
Pilate's troubled questioning;
then before the mob he stands,
calls for water, cleans his hands;
still they clamour, 'Crucify!' –
he condemns their king to die.

5 Christ is tried – yet so are we,
by his humble dignity:
pain and love upon his face
meet to show the way of grace:
all our judgement there he bore;
we are pardoned evermore.

Subject Index: B4, G2
77 77 77
Suggested Tunes: *Heathlands; Petra*

On the Night

1 On the night of his betrayal
when they were about to eat
Jesus knelt with towel and basin,
washing his disciples' feet.

2 On the night of his betrayal
special food had been prepared;
yet he brought a new fulfilment
to the ancient rite they shared.

3 On the night of his betrayal
taking wine and breaking bread,
he explained that he would suffer:
'This, my blood, for you is shed.'

4 On the night of his betrayal
Jesus had so much to say:
words to bring them reassurance
after he had gone away.

5 On the night of his betrayal
though aware of treachery,
still he chose to tread the pathway
into dark Gethsemane.

Subject Index: B4, I6
8 7 8 7
Suggested Tune: *Love Divine*

Open Our Eyes

1 Open our eyes to see
   the anguish of the poor –
   indignities untold
   where life is insecure;
      then may our ears discern your call
      to demonstrate your care for all.

2 Open our minds to grasp
   life's grim reality –
   how greed and power prolong
   the curse of poverty;
      and fill our mouths with words to speak,
      defending those whose voice is weak.

3 Open our hands to give,
   to serve through all our deeds,
   and let our strength be spent
   to meet our neighbours' needs;
      let love, not duty, be our guide:
      Lord, let our hearts be open wide!

Subject Index: H6, I4, J1
6 6 6 6 88
Suggested Tunes: *Bromborough; Love Unknown*

Journey

1 Pausing, we contemplate our journey:
how great the distance we have run!
So much has happened that has shaped us;
so much we, too, have said and done.
    Some of our memories are painful,
    some we shall treasure to the last:
    yet we are conscious of your leading
    along the pathways of our past.

2 How often we are at a crossroads,
needing to know which way to take:
whether to follow or ignore you –
such is the choice we have to make.
    Yet you have promised to be with us –
    no longer need we feel alone;
    help us to seize the present moment,
    making its full potential known.

3 Here on the threshold of the future,
laden with many hopes and fears,
turning our thoughts to new horizons,
we look ahead across the years.
    Who, though, can number their tomorrows
    on paths no human eye has scanned?
    May we continue on our journey
    holding – and held within – your hand.

1 Samuel 7:12; Psalm 31:15; Job 23:10; Joshua 24:15;
Matthew 4:19, 28:20; Mark 1:17; Ephesians 5:16;
Colossians 4:5; Hebrews 13:5; James 4:14-15; John 10:28-29
Subject Index: F5, H6, I1
9 8 9 8 D
Suggested Tune: *Rendez à Dieu*

Priest Eternal

1 Praise to Christ, the Lord incarnate,
   gift of God by human birth:
   he it is who came among us,
   shared our life and showed our worth;
      ours the turmoil he encountered,
      ours the fight he made his own;
      now within our hearts his Spirit
      makes his way of freedom known.

2 Praise to Christ, the Man of sorrows,
   tasting death for our release:
   his the cup of bitter anguish,
   ours the pardon, ours the peace;
      his the blood that seals forgiveness,
      ours the weight of guilt he bore –
      so by death and resurrection
      Christ has opened heaven's door.

3 Praise to Christ, the Priest eternal:
   still for us he intercedes;
   still he sees our pains and problems –
   how he understands our needs!
      Yesterday, today, forever,
      always he remains the same:
      pledged to bring us to the Father,
      strong in grace and free from blame.

1 John 4:9; Hebrews 2:14; 1 Peter 4:1; 2 Corinthians 3:17;
Isaiah 53:1; Hebrews 2:9; Luke 22:42; Colossians 1:14;
1 Peter 2:24; Hebrews 9:28; Revelation 4:1; Hebrews 9:24,
7:24-25, 4:15, 13:8; John 14:3; Jude 24
Subject Index: B1, H2, I2
8 7 8 7 D
Suggested Tunes: *God Commanded; Hope Park; Daily, Daily*
See also Appendix A

108

Christmas Bells

1 Ring aloud the Christmas bells –
joyful news their message tells:
news about a royal birth –
God has sent his Son to earth!

2 See the candles, burning bright –
Jesus came to give us light.
Light and life and truth and grace:
all are seen in Jesus' face.

3 Choosing gifts with special care
we express the love we share;
but the finest gift of all
is the Christ-child in the stall.

4 Beautiful the Christmas tree;
on a tree he died for me –
crucified, my sin he bore;
now he lives for evermore!

5 Sing the carols, loud and clear:
God our Saviour has come near.
Worship Christ, the newborn King –
life for all he's born to bring.

Subject Index: B2, F3, G2
77 77
Suggested Tunes: *Savannah; University College*
See also Appendix A

To Walk with You

1 Show me how to stand for justice:
　how to work for what is right,
　how to challenge false assumptions,
　how to walk within the light.
　　May I learn to share more freely
　　in a world so full of greed,
　　showing your immense compassion
　　by the life I choose to lead.

2 Teach my heart to treasure mercy,
　whether given or received –
　for my need has not diminished
　since the day I first believed:
　　let me seek no satisfaction
　　boasting of what I have done,
　　but rejoice that I am pardoned
　　and accepted in your Son.

3 Gladly I embrace a lifestyle
　modelled on your living word,
　in humility submitting
　to the truth which I have heard.
　　Make me conscious of your presence
　　every day, in all I do:
　　by your Spirit's gracious prompting
　　may I learn to walk with you.

Micah 6:8
Subject Index: F5, G3, H6
8 7 8 7 D
Suggested Tunes: *Abbot's Leigh; Hyfrydol; Praise*

To Savour Every Moment

1 Teach me, dear Lord, to savour every moment –
each precious hour, a gift which is unique –
for your unhurried guiding hand I cherish
and the contentment of your ways I seek.
When date and time demand my full attention
from frantic rushing let my heart be free,
that I may flow within your Spirit's rhythm
and live each minute just as it was meant to be.

2 But may I also glimpse the broader canvas –
to all my life, a purpose and a plan –
and let me hear again that voice which called me
before this world or time itself began.
So may your kingdom daily be my watchword
and may the pulse in all my life be praise,
across unfolding years and changing seasons,
until with you I walk through everlasting days.

Subject Index: F5, H6, J1
11 10 11 10 11 10 11 12
Suggested Tune: *Londonderry Air*

Forever in Your Grace

1 The changing of the seasons,
       the passing of the years,
   remind us just how swiftly
       a lifetime disappears;
   our frailty holds us captive –
       we grow, and age, and die –
   yet you remain for ever,
       eternal Lord most high.

2 We find that we inhabit
       a world of constant change:
   our parents' views and lifestyles
       our children find so strange.
   Let every generation
       its futile dreams pursue!
   Lord, you alone are changeless –
       our trust we place in you.

3 We gather to remember
       a course that has been run,
   a journey now completed,
       a battle fought and won.
   Be near us, Lord, in mercy,
       sustain us while we grieve;
   our hope is life eternal –
       your promise we believe.

4 You strengthen and direct us,
       our true and faithful guide;
   we turn to you for refuge;
       our courage you provide.
   Through Jesus you have shown us
       how much you love our race –
   so keep us, heavenly Father,
       forever in your grace.

Subject Index: A5, F5, G3
7 6 7 6 D
Suggested Tune: *Thornbury*
See also Appendix A
(Verses 1, 2 and 4 constitute a general hymn. By including verse 3
this becomes more specifically a hymn for a funeral or memorial
service.)

Our Guide

1 The choices which we face today
   remind us of our need to pray
   for wisdom, lest we miss the way:
      Lord, be our Guide!

2 We trace the pattern of the years,
   a patchwork quilt of joys and tears,
   and find one central thread appears:
      you were our Guide.

3 The future lies ahead, unknown,
   a land we cannot call our own:
   how can we tread its paths alone?
      We need a guide!

4 So, Lord, we pledge ourselves anew
   to put you first in all we do,
   throughout our lives to follow you –
      you are our Guide!

Subject Index: F5, G3, H4
888 4
Suggested Tune: *Es Ist Kein Tag (Meyer)*

The Gracious Invitation

1 The gracious invitation stands
   for any who will come;
   the Father runs with open arms
   to children heading home –
   and all who trudge with weary feet
   along life's dusty road
   receive at last a welcome chance
   to lose their heavy load.

2 No longer need we clothe our lives
   in garments soiled and torn
   when Christ gives robes of righteousness
   for what was old and worn:
   to those bereft of dignity
   and yearning to be whole,
   forgiveness brings the healing power
   which liberates the soul.

3 When all that busy lives produce
   is dry futility,
   we find in Christ the living source
   of full reality;
   and if, within our hearts, the truth
   is what we long to hear,
   the whisper of the Spirit comes
   as music to the ear.

4 Whoever looks for nourishment
   will find the table spread:
   the finest riches heaven holds,
   foretold in wine and bread.
   The banquet is for everyone,
   the greatest and the least:
   for all are called as honoured guests
   to come and join the feast!

Subject Index: G2, H1, I6
8 6 8 6 D (DCM)
Suggested Tunes: *Selfless Love; Kingsfold*

Coming Soon to Reign

1 The King is coming soon to reign
    in splendid resurrection power –
    although we cannot name the hour
we know he soon will come again.

2 Let all take note, and not forget
    that there will be a judgement day;
    God's mercy lengthens its delay –
his patience has not ended yet.

3 That day will bring both gain and loss
    as each receives a just reward:
    for saints, the welcome of their Lord,
but shame for all who spurned his cross.

4 Though now we taste mortality,
    his glorious promise we believe:
    when Jesus comes, we shall receive
new bodies for eternity.

5 Till then he tells us: watch and pray
    and in his service labour on;
    our time on earth will soon be gone –
for he may well return today!

Subject Index: B6, G2, J3
8 88 8 (LM)
Suggested Tunes: *Winchester New; Church Triumphant*

In Bread and Wine Encounter

1 The Lamb of God was faultless,
   with neither spot nor stain;
   for our forgiveness Jesus,
   the Lamb of God, was slain,
   and by his death he opened
   the way to God again:

   His body bruised and broken,
   his blood so freely poured:
   in bread and wine encounter
   the love of Christ our Lord.

2 The bread we break is sacred,
   the body of the Christ;
   and we are now his body –
   how highly we were priced!
   We eat with thankful hearts, for
   our Lord was sacrificed:

3 The cup we share reminds us
   what anguish he endured:
   he shed his blood to save us –
   our pardon he secured;
   his resurrection tells us
   acceptance is assured:

4 The life we live is holy,
   an offering of praise:
   his death has paid our ransom –
   how gracious are his ways!
   We live to serve our Saviour
   throughout our earthly days:

Subject Index: B4, H4, I6
7 6 7 6 7 6 refrain 7 6 7 6
Suggested Tune: *Berwick Street* (verses) and *St Alphege* (refrain)

The Lord Created Family

1 The Lord created family
   to make his kindness known:
   for when we care the way we ought
   our love reflects his own –
   a love which always reaches out
   to those who feel alone.

2 Give thanks for all the families
   which function as they should,
   whose members make it their delight
   to do each other good –
   for homes which truly demonstrate
   the Father's fatherhood.

3 But pray for those whose families
   are torn apart by strife –
   where pressure mounts, where love is scarce,
   where arguments are rife –
   that God will heal their brokenness
   and so enrich their life.

4 The Lord has made a family
   with members everywhere,
   and Jesus is the eldest Son,
   the one whose name we bear –
   whose words and life show holiness,
   a likeness we can share.

5 We are your Church, your family,
   the children of your grace:
   inspire us, Lord, to show this world
   the warmth of your embrace
   till all who long for wholeness find
   a welcome and a place.

Subject Index: H3, I3, J2
8 6 8 6 8 6
Suggested Tunes: *Brother James' Air; Morwellham*

To Trust and Persevere

1 The Lord is near: let patience be
    the hallmark of our lives.
As farmers wait to gain the yield
from plants they nurture in the field,
we yearn to see our King revealed
    at last, when he arrives.

2 He calls us to a way of life
    where grumbling has no place:
the loving Father we adore
is God all-holy, just and pure;
our trusting hearts are held secure
    entirely by his grace.

3 We share a priceless heritage
    with prophets from the past:
though made to suffer they were bold;
God's message they did not withhold;
may we, just like those saints of old,
    prove faithful to the last.

4 For this is what our calling means:
    to trust and persevere;
if even Job, in all his grief,
could spurn the lure of unbelief,
then how much greater our relief,
    to know: the Lord is near!

James 5:7-11; 1 Peter 1:17
Subject Index: G3, I2, J3
8 6 888 6
Suggested Tune: *Revelation*
See also Appendix B

The Son of God Is Here

1 The promised time arrives,
   the time of God's appointing –
   the time when One is born
   who bears the Lord's anointing.
      What prophets longed to see
      is finally made clear:
      for Jesus comes to earth
      and brings the Kingdom near.

2 Unnumbered angels sing
   in joyful acclamation,
   for Christ the Lord is born,
   the bringer of salvation:
      there in a manger lies
      the Lord of heaven and earth,
      who dignifies our life
      by sharing human birth.

3 He comes as David's Heir
   and Abraham's Descendant,
   yet takes no worldly throne
   with royal gold resplendent;
      though rulers seek him out
      to worship or to slay,
      no power devised on earth
      can take his crown away.

4 The way to God he shows
   to all who will receive him –
   what light and life are ours
   if we will but believe him!
      The Son of God is here,
      so full of truth and grace –
      God's glory is disclosed
      upon a human face.

Galatians 4:4; Mark 1:11, 15; 1 Peter 1:10; Luke 2:11-14;
Matthew 1:17, 2:1-2, 16; John 1:4, 12, 14, 14:6
Subject Index: B2, G2, J1
6 7 6 7 6 6 6 6
Suggested Tunes: *Gracias; Nun Danket*

At Pentecost

1 The Spirit came at Pentecost
in unexpected ways
and loosed believing hearts and tongues
in floods of prayer and praise.

2 Discernment, healing, prophecy –
so many gifts he brought,
but all to make the Church mature
in deed and word and thought.

3 He showed them love and joy and peace
to kindle their desire
for lives producing godly fruit
and purified by fire.

4 With grace and tenderness he came,
as gently as a dove,
and whispered, 'Children, you belong
within your Father's love.'

5 A faithful witness to the truth,
as Advocate he came;
he stirred the saints to rise and go,
the Gospel to proclaim.

6 To blow the breath of life upon
the dying and the lost,
to bring them to a second birth,
he came at Pentecost.

7 We need your Holy Spirit, Lord,
today as much as then –
so send him to us now, we pray,
to fill our hearts again!

Subject Index: C, H6, I1
8 6 8 6 (CM)
Suggested Tune: *St Fulbert*

From Far Away They Came

1 They were not from his people,
  they did not know his name;
  yet looking for the Saviour
  from far away they came:
    they saw his star appearing,
    a signal in the sky;
    their longings were rekindled,
    their hopes were lifted high.

2 They sought him in a palace,
  the place where kings reside:
  but Herod's greed and envy
  no challenge could abide.
    In Bethlehem they found him:
    how glad they were to see
    the Lord of all creation
    upon his mother's knee.

3 Then, bending low in worship
  before the infant King
  they offered him their treasures,
  the finest they could bring:
    who gives a baby incense
    or myrrh, or bars of gold?
    Yet these peculiar presents
    his life and death foretold.

4 And many still are searching
  with empty, aching hearts;
  in unexpected places
  his presence he imparts;
    the gifts we humbly offer
    he will receive and use –
    as Lord and King confess him –
    then go, proclaim the news!

Subject Index: B2, F5, G2
7 6 7 6 D
Suggested Tune: *Aurelia*

Living Bread

1 Together we proclaim
what Christ our Lord has done:
the greatest debt of all is paid,
the greatest triumph won.

2 From anguished, straining prayer
to mocking robe and thorn
to nails, a wooden cross and death
our weight of guilt was borne.

3 One body, and one loaf –
our hungry souls are fed;
by faith we find the strength we need
in Christ, the Living Bread.

4 The wine proclaims this truth:
his life-blood sets us free
to risk a life of faith and love,
secure in liberty.

5 He gives us bread and wine
and makes his life our own;
renewed, we go, resolved afresh
to make our Saviour known.

Subject Index: G2, H7, I6
6 6 8 6 (SM)
Suggested Tune: *Carlisle*

Prince of Peace

1 Travelling far on the Bethlehem road –
tiring for Mary, so heavy her load –
sent on the whim of an emperor in Rome:
'All shall pay taxes, so all shall go home!'
    An arrival foretold
    by the prophet of old
    for the Prince of Peace.

2 Told by the inn-keeper, 'No room to spare',
only a cattle-shed which they may share;
there he was born in the darkness of night,
coming to give us his marvellous light –
    what a place for a birth,
    for the coming to earth
    of the Prince of Peace.

3 Where can they lay him? The manger seems best;
Mary is weary and yearning for rest.
Sent by an angel, the shepherds appear,
eager to see that Messiah is here,
    for the infant who lay
    in the stall, on the hay
    is the Prince of Peace.

4 See the wise men and the treasures they bring;
hot on their heels is a murderous king:
Herod intends his own fears to allay –
innocent children his envy will slay,
    yet the child who must be
    now a young refugee
    is the Prince of Peace.

5 Over the manger a shadow appears –
suffering threatens to darken the years.
Pain and injustice his life soon will end:
this man to die on a cross they will send,
    but the man full of grace
    who was slain in our place
    is the Prince of Peace.

Subject Index: B2, G2, J1
10 10 10 10 66 5

A People Called by God

1 We are a people called by God,
    to be the heirs of grace –
ours is the task of making known
the way of mercy God has shown
    for all the human race.

2 Called to a royal, priestly role –
    disciples of the King!
As we recall what Christ endured,
we honour him, our Saviour-Lord:
    his praise we gladly sing.

3 Chosen to walk in holiness –
    a nation set apart –
living by grace, we do God's will,
and so the sacred call fulfil
    to be the pure in heart.

4 Christ teaches us his perfect law –
    and frees us to obey!
Since to the Lord we now belong,
we offer him, in life and song,
    our worship day by day.

1 Peter 2:9
Subject Index: H6, I2, J1
8 6 88 6
Suggested Tune: *Gatescarth*

With the Saints of Ages Past

1 We are called to stand together
with the saints of ages past,
with the patriarchs and prophets
in the faith they once held fast;
promises and hopes they treasured
now we find fulfilled at last!

2 Those whom Jesus called apostles
journeyed with him side by side,
heard his teaching, felt his power,
saw the way he lived and died;
then the news of resurrection
they delivered far and wide.

3 Through the intervening ages
round the world the Gospel spread:
faithful heralds took the message,
guided where the Spirit led;
so the body grew in stature,
serving Christ, its living Head.

4 Now in many tongues and cultures
songs of celebration ring;
millions who confess our Saviour
honour him as Lord and King
and, for courage, grace and guidance
every day their prayers they bring.

5 To each coming generation
tell the truth, persuade, explain,
till the time when time is ended,
till the Saviour comes again –
till the saints are all united
under Christ's eternal reign!

Subject Index: G2, I4, J1
8 7 8 7 8 7
Suggested Tunes: *Westminster Abbey; Mannheim*

Till That Day

1 We delight in the presence of God:
   it is good to come near to his throne,
   to remember his covenant love,
   to give thanks that he calls us his own.

2 Let us listen for all that he says –
   here the offer of life can be heard,
   for the truth brings the freedom we crave
   when our lives are aligned with his word.

3 He will judge every nation on earth,
   and the clamour of battle will cease
   when the weapons of war are destroyed
   in the light of his justice and peace.

4 Till that day, when his word is fulfilled,
   he has promised to keep us secure;
   let us faithfully walk with the Lord
   and confess him the God we adore!

Micah 4:2-5
Subject Index: F5, H6, J1
9 9 9 9

126

Resurrection Day

1 We hear the words which echoed round the tomb:
  'The stone stands empty where his body lay.'
  The barren grave is changed into a womb –
  Christ lives on this, the resurrection day!

2 Here is the flame which sets our lives ablaze –
  to think that heaven's doors are open now!
  And so with hearts which overflow with praise
  before the risen Son of God we bow.

3 A royal call to service we receive:
  we are the witnesses he wants to use,
  for who can hear the message and believe,
  without a messenger to tell the news?

4 His promise spells the end of all our fear,
  with hope which even death cannot destroy:
  for, by his Spirit, Christ is ever near,
  and dark despair is turned to lasting joy.

5 Now by the Wind the sound is borne along
  till far and wide the strains of laughter ring
  and every nation hears at last the song
  that Jesus died and rose and reigns as King.

Subject Index: B5, F3, H7
10 10 10 10
Suggested Tune: *Woodlands*

This Joyous Certainty

1 What joy your presence gives us, Lord:
  for where you make your home,
  eternal pleasures come –
and how we love to hear your voice,
  to find the strength we need
  as on your word we feed.

2 It is by faith that you are known,
  revealed to childlike eyes,
  though not the worldly-wise –
and you have chosen us by name!
  This joyous certainty
  is our security!

3 If now the path we tread is rough,
  whatever trials we find
  will soon be left behind:
your gracious care will guide us through
  to firm and level ground
  where life and joy abound.

4 We stand where once the prophets stood,
  who suffered for their Lord
  and won a great reward:
if we are slandered for your sake,
  in you we have a joy
  no hardship can destroy.

5 So, Lord, we focus on your Son,
  who saw beyond the loss
  of death upon the cross;
through his unblemished righteousness
  this gift is ours to share:
  your joy, beyond compare!

Psalm 16:11; Jeremiah 15:16; Luke 10:20, 21; Isaiah 43:1;
John 16:20; Matthew 5:11-12; 1 Peter 5:10; Hebrews 12:2, 1:9
Subject Index: F2, H6, I1
8 66 D
See also Appendix B

Whatever Bleakness

1 What kind of choice is this
   for anyone to face:
   to flee and live – or stay and die
   in someone else's place?

2 Such bitter pain it brings –
   a kiss, and yet so cold!
   Betrayed by one he called a friend,
   for silver he is sold.

3 A fiction of a trial:
   a killer they release
   while in a tangled web of lies
   they snare the Prince of Peace.

4 They rant, and spit, and taunt;
   they mock with robe and thorn –
   he hangs, deprived of dignity
   amid unending scorn.

5 A heavy load he bears,
   unseen by mortal eyes:
   our brokenness he makes his own
   as in our place he dies.

6 What kind of love is this?
   When life is at its worst,
   whatever bleakness mars my path,
   my Saviour felt it first.

Subject Index: B4, G1, H2
6 6 8 6 (SM)
Suggested Tune: *St Thomas*

The Humble King

1 What kind of reign is this,
    provoking such a scene?
    These crowds, the palms, the cloaks, the songs:
    what can they mean?
    God's Chosen One arrives,
    and loud hosannas ring
    as on a donkey's foal he rides,
    the humble King.

2 But with a heavy heart
    this Prince of Peace has come,
    his eyes awash with tears for lost
    Jerusalem –
    and in the temple courts
    his holy anger burns:
    the greedy money-changers' stalls
    he overturns.

3 This promised, rightful Heir,
    by prophets long foretold,
    brings teaching and authority
    both clear and bold;
    the leaders whom he chides
    respond with rage and fear –
    they plot his fate; the crisis grows;
    the cross looms near.

4 They want his blood, he knows,
    and he will be betrayed –
    there in the darkened olive-grove
    his choice is made:
    he takes the bitter cup
    with all it will entail,
    resolved to face the agonies
    of thorn and nail.

5 What kind of reign is this,
    fulfilled at such a price:
    a King who freely gives himself
    in sacrifice!
    With wonder we recall
    the path our Saviour trod,
    acknowledging the risen Christ
    our Lord and God.

Luke 19:35-38; Mark 11:8-10; Isaiah 9:6; Luke 19:42; Mark 11:15;
John 2:15-17; Luke 20:14, 26, 19:48, 20:19, 22:2; Mark 14:18, 21;
John 18:1; Matthew 26:36; Hebrews 12:2; John 19:30, 20:28

Subject Index: B3, J1   6 6 8 4 D   Suggested Tune: *Leoni*

Forgiven All

1 What priceless treasures fill the hearts
of all who are forgiven much,
for grace is like the finest gold
to those who feel God's loving touch:
a debt removed, a heart made pure,
a pardon sealed for evermore!

2 Forgiveness is the gift of God
when harsher treatment would be right;
the words which calm our gnawing guilt
reveal the Father's chief delight –
to tame and turn the rebel soul,
to make the broken sinner whole.

3 If we deny our need of grace
what foolish pride our words betray,
since all the wrongs which we confess
the blood of Christ will clean away:
here justice and compassion meet –
and here forgiveness is complete.

4 Released from sin's oppressive grasp,
we make the way of grace our own
as to each other we extend
a pardon such as we have known:
forgiven all, forever free:
what higher calling could there be?

Psalm 32:1-2; Micah 7:18; Isaiah 43:25; Jeremiah 31:34;
1 John 1:8-9; Romans 6:14, 18; Ephesians 4:32
Subject Index: G2, H2, I2
8 8 8 8 88
Suggested Tune: *Melita*

Unless You Help Me

1 When anxious thoughts assail my mind,
  when I begin to doubt your care,
  when gloom and sorrow flood my soul,
  I bring my fears to you, my God, in prayer.

2 I call to you to answer soon,
  to turn my darkness into light,
  for life can be a battlefield –
  unless you help me, I shall lose the fight!

3 Yet in your endless love I trust,
  in your salvation I rejoice:
  because you have been good to me
  I offer you my praise with heart and voice.

Psalm 13
Subject Index: F1, H3, J2
8 8 8 10
Suggested Tune: *Bardfield Sailing*

When Circumstances

1 When circumstances make my life
  too hard to understand,
  no doubt or fear, no pain or strife,
  can snatch me from God's hand.

2 In valleys where the path is steep,
  with shadows dark and long,
  I know the Shepherd leads his sheep –
  his grace will keep me strong.

3 Though sorrow and perplexity
  are often what I feel,
  Gethsemane and Calvary
  affirm God's love is real.

4 It is enough for me to know
  his promise and his care:
  wherever on life's path I go
  my Saviour will be there.

Subject Index: G3, H2, J2
8 6 8 6 (CM)
Suggested Tunes: *Shepherd Boy's Song; Contemplation*
See also Appendix A

Where Senses Fade

1 When shape and colour flood my sight,
   when light and beauty draw my gaze,
   great God, may what my eyes discern
   direct my thoughts to you in praise.

2 Let every whisper, word and cry,
   let every note and tune and chord,
   contain an echo of the call
   which drew me first to you, my Lord.

3 What rich aromas fill the air!
   What flavours charm the appetite!
   Yet each of these is but a gift
   from you, who are my true delight.

4 The softness of a tender touch,
   the firmness of the path I tread –
   may neither captivate my soul
   when I should reach for you instead.

5 So let my spirit soar to realms
   where senses fade, where faith endures –
   until, most holy One-yet-Three,
   my heart and soul are truly yours.

Subject Index: F5, H6, J2
8 8 8 8 (LM)
Suggested Tune: *Church Triumphant*

Let Us Be Signals

1 When you spoke and shaped creation
   you designed it to be good:
   galaxies and ecosystems
   functioned as you said they should.
   By your living Word of power
   you sustain the cosmos, still:
       God of splendour, how we marvel
       at your vast creative skill.

2 But the people you appointed
   to the care of what you made
   disregarded your instruction,
   spurned the truth, and disobeyed;
   and we all, by our behaviour,
   frequently endorse that choice –
       God of grace, we need your pardon
       for our deafness to your voice.

3 When the future seems so threatened
   by the evils of our race;
   when pollution, war and famine
   are the issues we must face;
   when in our lives your reflection
   is distorted, blurred or cracked,
       God of wholeness, may your wisdom
       be a light our hearts refract.

4 Teach us, then, to treat creation
   with attention and respect,
   not to scorn its rich resources
   by abuse or cool neglect:
   you who formed this planet's beauty
   lent its wealth for all to share:
       God of hope, let us be signals
       of your rule and of your care.

Subject Index: A2, F5, J1
8 7 8 7 D
Suggested Tunes: *Hope Park; Bethany*

Where Shadows

1 Where shadows once were found,
  where death was loathed and feared,
  where men and women lived in gloom
  a light has now appeared.

2 To all our darkest paths
  the light has found a way;
  and nor can darkness master it –
  the light has come to stay.

3 This light which we have seen
  is Christ, and Christ alone:
  by truth and grace the living Light
  has made the Father known.

4 The brightness we had lost
  in Christ is now restored:
  believing human hearts reflect
  the splendour of the Lord.

5 So in our daily lives
  let grace and truth abound;
  Lord, by your Spirit shine through us
  where shadows once were found.

Isaiah 9:2; John 1:5, 14; 2 Corinthians 3:18
Subject Index: B2, F5, H6
6 6 8 6 (SM)
Suggested Tunes: *Sandys; Holyrood*

Love's Awful Splendour

1 Who can come into the presence
of the Lord, the holy King?
Sacrifices fit to please him
which of us could ever bring?
Who has felt his gracious cleansing?
Who has hands and heart made pure?
Only those who know his mercy
meet with God and stand secure.

2 He is Lord of endless glory,
living in unfading light;
love eternal is his splendour,
love so pure, a flame so bright.
Love so full and all-embracing
feels the pain of every loss:
yearning meets with deepest anguish,
passions merging at the cross.

3 Born among us as a baby,
God became a refugee,
then, arrested, tried and sentenced,
tasted death's indignity.
Still he feels the anguished achings
of the hungry and oppressed;
still he stands with those ill-treated,
mocked, abused and dispossessed.

4 Who can leave his holy presence
unaffected by the pain?
Who can face love's awful splendour
and ignore a call so plain?
Help us, Lord, to feel your sorrow;
your compassion may we share –
so that we extend your kingdom
by the grief and love we bear!

Subject Index: A3, G1, J2
8 7 8 7 D
Suggested Tunes: *Hyfrydol; Bethany*

My Trust and Triumph

1 Within my heart a desert lies –
  an empty land, a barren place –
  and like a traveller racked with thirst
  I long for you, the God of grace.

2 Your power and glory once I knew:
  those memories still enthral my mind –
  they tell me that your presence brings
  a feast for hungry souls to find.

3 When anxious thoughts disrupt my sleep,
  to your unfailing care I cling
  till, lifted by your tender strength,
  my weary spirit starts to sing.

4 Whatever troubles lie ahead,
  your constant love will see me through:
  my God, my joy, I sing your praise –
  my trust and triumph are in you.

Psalm 63
Subject Index: F1, G3, H3
8 8 8 8 (LM)
Suggested Tunes: *Church Triumphant; O Righteous Lord*

Anointed by Tranquillity

1 Within the busy rush of life
    I find a resting-place:
  when I submit to Christ my Lord
    and let him set my pace
  he shows the way that I should take
    whatever trials I face.

2 Amid the choices I must make
    and duties that increase
  he comes to calm my anxious thoughts,
    to make the turmoil cease;
  as in his presence I remain
    he guides me into peace.

3 The timeless, all-sufficient God
    my every longing knows
  and daily he refreshes me
    with joy which overflows;
  anointed by tranquillity
    my strength to serve him grows.

4 My Saviour bids me walk with him
    and follow all his ways –
  his plan for me is fruitfulness
    throughout my earthly days,
  since now and evermore I live
    beneath his loving gaze.

Subject Index: A4, G1, H6
8 6 8 6 8 6
Suggested Tunes: *Morden; Brother James' Air*
See also Appendix A

God Is for Us

1 Yes, God is for us! Who could doubt
the measure of his care?
He gives us all he has in Christ,
the Son he did not spare:
through him, God's all-surpassing gift,
so much is ours to share!

2 No condemnation threatens those
whom God has justified,
and slander which maligns his saints
the Lord will sweep aside –
the risen Saviour, by his prayer,
guards all for whom he died.

3 So if our lives are overturned,
our plans all run aground,
or if we find ourselves at risk
from perils all around –
despite these trials, within our hearts
the love of Christ is found.

4 Now more than conquerors through that love,
we triumph, come what may:
no time, no space, nor any powers
can steal his love away –
secure in Christ, secure in God,
for ever we shall stay.

Romans 8:31-39
Subject Index: G1, H5, I2
8 6 8 6 8 6
Suggested Tunes: *Sheltered Dale; Tynemouth*
See also Appendix B

You Make the Father Known

1 You are the Bread of Life
 which feeds the hungry soul;
 your body, broken on the cross,
 was torn to make us whole.
 Your flesh is food so real,
 your blood is drink indeed –
 Lord Jesus, in your life we find
 the nourishment we need.

2 You are the Prince of Peace,
 the one who offers rest
 for troubled, weary, aching hearts
 by burdens long oppressed.
 You will not weigh us down,
 our load you humbly bear –
 how glad we are to learn your ways,
 your easy yoke to share.

3 You are the only Way,
 the Truth whom we believe,
 and those who place their trust in you
 eternal life receive.
 You make the Father known,
 his glory lights your face –
 his splendour you reveal to us
 in mercy, truth and grace.

John 6:48, 55-56; Isaiah 9:6; Matthew 11:28-30;
John 14:6-7, 1:17-18
Subject Index: B1, F5, H2
6 6 8 6 D (DSM)
Suggested Tune: *Diademata*

Lord Jesus Christ, We Bow

1 You are the Source of all creation –
   we owe to you our very birth!
   When time itself was uncreated
   your wisdom planned both heavens and earth;
   still in your hand you hold the cosmos,
   your mighty word sustains it all –
   Lord Jesus Christ, we bow in worship:
   humbly before your throne we fall.

2 You are the Focus of creation:
   all things were made for your delight;
   endless dominion is your glory,
   endless authority, your right.
   We find our freedom and fulfilment
   serving where you assign our place –
   Lord Jesus Christ, we bow in worship,
   thrilled to belong to you by grace.

3 You are the Hope of all creation,
   making the Father's purpose known:
   pardon, and wholeness, and a future –
   these we can find in you alone;
   for by your death and resurrection
   you shape this universe anew –
   Lord Jesus Christ, we bow in worship,
   wholly and gladly trusting you.

Subject Index: B1, I2, J2
9 8 9 8 D
Suggested Tune: *Rendez à Dieu*

This Generous Care

1 You give us so much: a world to enjoy,
  such treasures to find, such skills to employ:
  the lavish abundance of all that you give
  invites us to flourish, not merely to live!

2 You give us your all: in Christ you have shown
  the price you would pay to make us your own:
  our debts have been cleared by his death on the cross –
  now heaven stands open: our gain from his loss.

3 As children of grace, with all who believe
  we bring you our thanks for all we receive –
  yet who can imagine how far it extends,
  this generous care which you show to your friends?

4 Then what can we do to answer your call,
  but give you our first, our best and our all?
  Our money, our time and our talents we bring –
  our lives as a love-gift to honour our King.

Subject Index: F4, G3, I3
10 10 11 11
Suggested Tune: *Laudate Dominum* (Parry)

Eternal Lover

1 You have won me with a love
far surpassing mere emotion –
let my heart be yours alone,
overflowing with devotion.

2 For you hold me in a bond
neither earth nor hell can sever:
in my soul there shines a light
which I know will blaze for ever.

3 Let your splendour fill my thoughts,
capture my imagination,
till my mind, with pure delight,
turns to you in adoration.

4 All the strength which I possess,
may I spend it for your pleasure:
every sinew, muscle, nerve,
every skill be yours to treasure.

5 Nothing else can satisfy
like the joys which I discover
when I give my all to you,
gracious God, eternal Lover.

Mark 12:30
Subject Index: F2, G1, H4
7 8 7 8
Suggested Tune: *Asthall*

Resurrection Breakfast

1 You stood there on the shoreline
 and waited in the dawn
 to share with your disciples
 the newness of the morn;
  be with us now, Lord Jesus,
  and make your presence known:
  in resurrection power
  declare today your own.

2 When hours of tiring labour
 had brought them scant reward,
 in your immense provision
 they recognised their Lord;
  when drudgery seems endless,
  demeaning all our skill,
  let this be our contentment:
  to know and do your will.

3 On bread and fish they feasted
 around a charcoal fire:
 that resurrection breakfast
 was all they could desire!
  Like them, may we discover
  the joy which never ends
  when you, the King of glory,
  count us among your friends.

4 Where Simon Peter languished
 in guilt and burning shame,
 you spoke of restoration,
 and not of endless blame;
  where sin and failure haunt us,
  remind us what is true:
  that we are now forgiven
  and called to follow you.

John 21
Subject Index: B5, F5, H6
7 6 7 6 D
Suggested Tunes: *Thornbury; Wolvercote*

Appendixes and Indexes

Appendix A: Inclusive Language Variations

(See the Introduction for notes relating to these variations to the standard texts.)

No	v.l	Alternative Text
2	5.3	To you, our Saviour, our Delight,
4	3.3	to disregard such wisdom
15	3.4	make us strong and make us wise!
17	3.2-4	Hear the command to repent and believe!
		Children of dust in God's glory may share,
		penitent rebels, God's favour receive.
21	2.4	when the voice from heaven sounded?
27	3.4	the One who comes to recreate
	3.6	the song God's new creation sings!
33	1.6	to know the One who sees us
	3.4-7	give thanks to the Lord
		who knows our every feeling
		and speaks in grace, revealing
		encouragement and healing –
41	1.1	Give thanks to the Lord for that marvellous gift:
	2.1-4	How great was the depth of the love of the Lord,
		who gave us the Son, at unspeakable cost –
		the riches of heaven were willingly spent
		fulfilling God's yearning to rescue the lost.
54	4.5	in whose sovereign will you lead
57	2.1	We trust the One whose strong, creative word
	2.3	the God who holds unnumbered galaxies
	2.4	but yearns, our inmost hearts to own.
66	1.2	one good, eternal plan
	2.1	God fashions for our benefit

No	v.l	Alternative Text
	3.3	for those God chose were called aside,
	3.4	and being called, were justified
75	3.2	is risen now, and glorified
76	1.2-4	a love from God alone,
		the hallmark of the children
		whom God delights to own.
	2.6	by giving us the Son:
	3.5	for though we cannot prove it
	3.7	yet God is truly present
80	2.2	held in a loving, fatherly embrace;
	2.3	God's care remains, whatever trials we face:
	3.3	eternal splendour we shall see displayed:
	4.3	whose perfect likeness one day we shall share:
	5.2	such precious gifts of life and joy abound –
81	3.4	which will not honour Christ in everything.
100	2.5	The precious Son of God is he,
101	2.3	Jesus came with love and power,
	5.6	ever to be glorified!
107	3.7	pledged to bring us home to heaven,
108	1.4	God the Son has come to earth!
111	4.7	so keep us, God of mercy,
132	2.3-4	I know the Shepherd leads the sheep with grace which keeps us strong.
	4.2	God's promise and God's care:
138	3.3	and every day refreshes me
	3.6	my strength for service grows.

Appendix B: Two Series of Texts

This appendix lists two sets of texts which were written as series. The first is eight texts based on Romans 8, aiming to cover the whole chapter; these were written over a period of some months. The second set is based on the fruit of the Spirit, from Galatians 5.

Eight texts from Romans 8

vv 1-4	No condemnation holds us now	99
vv 5-9	I choose to set my thoughts the way	64
vv 9-14	For believing hearts, a gift	31
vv 14-17	Children of God himself	16
vv 18-25	In the face of present sufferings	69
vv 26-27	Holy Spirit, will you be	54
vv 28-30	In all things God is working out	66
vv 31-39	Yes, God is for us! Who could doubt	139

Nine texts from the fruit of the Spirit (Galatians 5:22-23)

Love	Let love be found among us	76
Joy	What joy your presence gives us, Lord	127
Peace	Christ is our peace! For Christ himself	20
Patience	The Lord is near: let patience be	117
Kindness	My Father, full of endless love	96
Goodness	God to whom all praise belongs	47
Meekness	Jesus, you have shown us how	74
Faithfulness	Incarnate Word, you spoke the truth	68
Self-control	Lord Jesus, by your mercy	88

Appendix C: Sources of Suggested Tunes

The following list is not exhaustive, but is designed to indicate one or more books in which the named tunes can be found. Many of these tunes will also be found in numerous other standard hymnals; and in the case of the newer hymnals in this list, many standard tunes will be found but are not listed here. Unpublished tunes are available from Martin Leckebusch via Kevin Mayhew.

(Ahead of us) by		God Commanded	SG
A. Griffith	P	Gott Will's Machen	HOAN, HTC, H&P
Abbot's Leigh	HOAN, HTC, H&P	Gracias	HOAN, HTC, H&P
Aberystwyth	HOAN, HTC, H&P	Griffin's Brook	H&P
Abridge	HOAN, HTC, H&P	Hale Bank	Unpublished tune by Ian Sharp
Ach Gott und Herr	HOAN, HTC, H&P	Heathlands	HOAN, HTC, H&P, P
Addison's (London)	HOAN, H&P	Hollingside	HTC, H&P
Agincourt	SG	Holyrood	HOAN, HTC
Aigburth Vale	Unpublished tune by Ian Sharp	Hope Park	NS, SG
Albano	HOAN, HTC	Hyfrydol	HOAN, NS, HTC, H&P
All for Jesus	HOAN, NS, HTC, H&P	Hymn to Freedom	Unpublished adaptation
All Hallows (Brown)	CP		from *Hymn to Freedom* by Oscar
All Saints	HOAN, SG, HTC, H&P		Peterson
Alleluia	HOAN, HTC	Ibstone	HOAN, SG, HTC, H&P, P
Angel Voices	HOAN, HTC, H&P	In Babilone	HTC
Angelus	HOAN, HTC, H&P	Intercessor	H&P
Arfon	SG, HTC	Jerusalem	HOAN, HTC
Asthall	HTC	Kilve	NS
Aurelia	HOAN, HTC, H&P	Kingsfold	HOAN, NS, HTC, H&P
Austria	HOAN, NS, HTC, H&P	Latvia	SG
Bardfield Sailing	Unpublished tune by Ian Sharp	Laudate Dominum	
Barnard Gate	SG, HTC	(Parry)	HOAN, HTC, H&P
Belmont	HOAN, HTC, H&P	Leoni	HOAN, HTC, H&P
Berwick Street	SP	Little Cornard	HOAN, HTC, H&P
Bethany	H&P	Little Heath	HTC, P
Blaenwern	HOAN, NS, HTC, H&P	Llangloffan	H&P
Blessed Assurance	HOAN, H&P	Londonderry Air	HOAN, HTC, H&P, P
Bolsterstone	NS	Longfield	Unpublished tune by Ian Sharp
Bow Brickhill	HOAN, HTC, H&P	Lord of Love	HTC
Bromborough	NS	Love Divine	HOAN, HTC, H&P
Brother James' Air	HTC	Love Unknown	HOAN, NS, HTC, H&P
Bunessan	HOAN, HTC, H&P	Mannheim	HOAN, HTC, H&P
Burgess Hill	Unpublished tune by Ian Sharp	Martyrdom	HOAN, HTC, H&P
Calon Lân	NS, SG, HTC, H&P	Melita	HOAN, HTC, H&P
Carlisle	HOAN, HTC, H&P	Montgomery	HOAN, HTC
Chedworth	SG, HTC	Morden	SG, HTC, P
Childhood	HOAN	Morning Light	HOAN, HTC, H&P
Church Triumphant	HOAN, HTC, H&P	Morwellham	CP
Contemplation	HOAN, HTC, H&P	Neander	HOAN, HTC, H&P
Cottingham	Unpublished tune by Ian Sharp	Nettleton	H&P, P
Crüger (Herrnhut)	HOAN, HTC, H&P	Noel	HOAN, HTC, H&P
Cuckfield	P	Normandy (Basque)	H&P
Daily, Daily	HOAN	Northover	H&P
Deepcar	NS	Nun Danket	HOAN, HTC, H&P, P
Deerhurst	HOAN	O Perfect Love	HOAN, HTC, H&P
Diademata	HOAN, NS, H&P	O Righteous Lord	SG
Dix	HOAN, HTC, H&P	Ode to Joy	HOAN, NS, HTC
Duke Street	HOAN, HTC, H&P	Penlan	HOAN, HTC, H&P
Ebenezer		Petra	HOAN, HTC, H&P
(Ton-y-Botel)	HOAN, HTC, H&P	Praise	P
Edwen	Unpublished tune by Ian Sharp	Quam Dilecta	HOAN, HTC
Ellacombe	HOAN, HTC, H&P	Ratisbon	HOAN, HTC, H&P
Engleberg	HOAN, NS, HTC, H&P	Rendez à Dieu	HOAN, HTC, H&P
Epiphany		Revelation	HTC
(Epiphany Hymn)	HOAN, NS, SG, HTC, H&P	Sacrifice	Unpublished tune by Ian Sharp
Es Ist Kein Tag (Meyer)	H&P	Salzburg (Hintze)	HOAN, H&P
Finlandia	HOAN, NS, HTC	Sandys	HOAN, HTC, H&P
Framlingham	HTC	Savannah	HOAN, HTC, H&P
Gasquet Hall	NS	Selfless Love	HTC, P
Gatescarth	HTC, H&P	Sheltered Dale	H&P
Go Forth	HTC, H&P	Shepherd Boy's Song	SG, H&P

Sine Nomine	HOAN, HTC, H&P
Slane	HOAN, NS, HTC, H&P
Song 1	HOAN, HTC, H&P
St Agnes (Dykes)	HOAN, HTC, H&P
St Albinus	HOAN, HTC, H&P
St Alphege	HOAN, HTC
St Andrew (Thorne)	HOAN, HTC
St Catherine (Tynemouth)	HOAN, HTC, H&P
St Edmund	HOAN, HTC
St Fulbert	HOAN, HTC, H&P
St George's Windsor	HOAN, HTC, H&P
St Leonard's (Gould)	HOAN, HTC, H&P
St Magnus	HOAN, HTC, H&P
St Margaret	HOAN, HTC, P
St Matthew	HOAN, H&P
St Thomas	HOAN, HTC, H&P
Stowey	HOAN, HTC
Stuttgart	HOAN, HTC, H&P
Sussex	HOAN, HTC, H&P
Sutton Manor	Unpublished tune by Ian Sharp
Swahili	HOAN
Symphony No 1 – Brahms	Unpublished adaptation from Symphony No 1 by Johannes Brahms

Thaxted	HOAN, HTC
The Promise	NS
The Staff of Faith	SG, H&P, P
The Vines	SG
Thornbury	HOAN, NS, HTC, H&P
Trentham	HOAN
Tynemouth	CP
University College	HOAN, HTC, H&P
Walsall	HTC
Westminster Abbey	HOAN, SG, HTC, H&P
Winchester New	HOAN, HTC, H&P
Wolvercote	HOAN, HTC, H&P
Woodlands	HOAN, NS, HTC, H&P
Wootton Bassett	Unpublished tune by Ian Sharp

Key

HOAN	Hymns Old and New
NS	New Start Hymns and Songs
SG	Sing Glory
HTC	Hymns for Today's Church
H&P	Hymns & Psalms
P	Praise!
CP	Congregational Praise
SP	Songs of Praise

Metrical Index

Note: an asterisk (*) denotes a tune which can be used only by combining or dividing verses of the text.

Metre	No	First line	Tune(s)
4 6 8 5 4 8 8 6	35	Freedom, we pray	*Hymn to Freedom*
5 5 5 4 D	46	God our provider	*Bunessan*
5 5 5 5 D	95	More than words can say	*Longfield*
6 5 8 5 D	45	God of our salvation	*Swahili (adapted)*
6 6 6 6	97	My Lord, you called my name	*Ibstone, Quam Dilecta*
6 6 6 6 44 6 6	39	Give glory to Jesus	*Symphony No 1 – Brahms*
6 6 6 6 88	16	Children of God himself	*Little Cornard*
	78	Let us exalt our King	*Little Cornard*
	105	Open our eyes to see	*Bromborough, Love Unknown*
6 6 8 4 D	129	What kind of reign is this	*Leoni*
6 6 8 6 (SM)	3	A crown of piercing thorns	*St Thomas*
	60	How privileged we are	*Carlisle, Trentham*
	121	Together we proclaim	*Carlisle*
	128	What kind of choice is this	*St Thomas*
	135	Where shadows once were found	*Sandys, Holyrood*
6 6 8 6 D (DSM)	140	You are the Bread of life	*Diademata*
6 7 6 7 6 6 6 6	118	The promised time arrives	*Gracias, Nun Danket*
7 5 7 5 777 7	33	For riches of salvation	*Burgess Hill*
7 66 D	18	Christian soldiers in the fight	*Cuckfield*
7 6 7 6	88	Lord Jesus, by your mercy	*St Alphege*
7 6 7 6 7 6 refr. 7 6 7 6	115	The Lamb of God was faultless	*Berwick Street/St Alphege*
7 6 7 6 D	4	A depth of satisfaction	*Crüger (Herrnhut), Ellacombe*
	53	He spoke at the beginning	*Aurelia, Morning Light*
	76	Let love be found among us	*Wolvercote, Penlan, Nettleton*
	111	The changing of the seasons	*Thornbury*
	120	They were not from his people	*Aurelia*
	144	You stood there on the shoreline	*Thornbury, Wolvercote*
7 6 7 6 Triple	32	For every word which feeds us	*Thaxted*
7 6 7 7	38	From the depths my soul cries out	*Sutton Manor*
7 6 8 6 D	56	How could you leave the splendour	*Llangloffan*
	62	How urgent is the summons	*Llangloffan, St Margaret*
7 7 7 7	108	Ring aloud the Christmas bells	*Savannah, University College*
7 7 7 7 7 7	31	For believing hearts, a gift	*Dix*
	54	Holy Spirit, will you be	*Arfon, Petra*
	87	Lord, I gladly trust in you	*Petra, Ratisbon*
	103	One whose heart is hard as steel	*Heathlands, Petra*
7 7 7 7 D	12	Born of Adam's rebel race	*Hollingside*

Scriptural Index

Church Year Index

Subject Index

Thematic Index

Index of Titles and First Lines

First lines are in ordinary type; titles in italics.
Titles are not included where they match the opening of the first line.